HIGH BLOOD PRESSURE
SPECIAL DIET COOKBOOK

**Delicious low-salt recipes that are
calorie controlled for weight reduction**

Maggie Pannell

Thorsons
An Imprint of HarperCollins*Publishers*

Thorsons
An Imprint of HarperCollins*Publishers*

Thorsons
An Imprint of HarperCollins*Publishers*
77–85 Fulham Palace Road,
Hammersmith, London W6 8JB

Published by Thorsons 1991
10 9 8 7 6 5 4 3 2

Copyright © Maggie Pannell 1991

Maggie Pannell asserts the moral right to be
identified as the author of this work

A catalogue record for this book is available
from the British Library

ISBN 0 7225 2236 3

Printed in Great Britain by The Bath Press,
Avon

CONTENTS

THANKS AND DEDICATION

To my husband, Peter, who every evening for many months, dined on whatever I happened to be testing that day.

An objective taster is vital and his constructive comments, continuous support and encouragement were invaluable to me in the writing of this book.

I would also like to express my warm gratitude to Janet Penfound (B.Sc., SRD) for her much appreciated help and advice, and my thanks to my good friend, Maire Evans who assisted with the American conversions.

INTRODUCTION

First and foremost, this is not a book just for people with high blood pressure or, to give it the correct medical name, hypertension. It's a book for anyone and everyone who cares about what they eat and the preventative diet measures they can take to look after their health. I stress this point because the problem with high blood pressure is that, unless you have a regular medical check-up or have a particular reason or condition that requires your blood pressure to be measured, you won't know whether you have high blood pressure or not. There are frequently no symptoms, although headaches, dizzy spells and tiredness may sometimes be an indication. Having said that, most people who have high blood pressure feel quite well and, sadly, it is only when they have a stroke or heart attack that the alarm bells ring by which time it may be too late! It makes sense therefore to try and prevent this situation from arising in the first place.

There are no clear cut, direct causes of hypertension — there are a number of contributing factors. Some of these are outside our control, but sensible diet and keeping weight down are important measures that you can actively and positively do something about.

This does not mean following a boring, unappetizing, cranky diet which the family won't enjoy eating or that you will find difficult to stick to. Personally I don't believe in strict regimes. If recipes are not practical to make or enjoyable to eat, there's little chance of a diet being effective. Naturally it's necessary to make some adjustments, but this doesn't mean sacrificing flavour or variety — in fact quite the opposite. You can develop a renewed interest in shopping, cooking and eating, and hopefully enjoy your meals much more than before. But before going into more detail about the diet and recipes, you may like to know a little more about the condition itself.

WHAT IS HIGH BLOOD PRESSURE?

We all have blood pressure. It is simply a measure of the amount of force needed to be applied by the heart to drive blood through the arteries to all the organs and tissues in the body. It varies depending upon what you're doing. For example, exercise, excitement, anger and anxiety will all make the heart beat faster and therefore increase blood pressure. If you're sitting down quietly and relaxed, blood pressure drops. These temporary ups–and–downs are normal. The problem for sufferers of hypertension is that the blood pressure remains high and, in time, this damages the blood vessels and interferes with the blood flow to vital organs. If it is not detected, kidney failure, heart disease, and strokes can follow.

WHAT CAUSES IT?

The exact way in which high blood pressure develops is not properly under-stood but there are a number of risk factors and contributing causes. It is a common condition, affecting about one in seven people. Or, to be more precise, about a quarter of middle-aged adults in Britain, for instance, have blood pressure over the safe, normal level of 140/90. However, certain people are more likely to be affected and should therefore have their blood pressure checked regularly — ideally once a year. Higher risk groups include:

- Those with a family history of high blood pressure (or heart disease or stroke).
- Those with diabetes. Diabetics have an increased risk of having a heart attack and, therefore, need to take especially good care of their health.

- The male sex generally. A man with high blood pressure is twice as likely to have a heart attack as a man with normal blood pressure. However, after the menopause, women catch up on rates of heart attacks.

Hypertension is rare in young people, but as you get older the blood vessels become less resilient and blood pressure frequently rises to maintain circulation. So, over 40 years of age, blood pressure is likely to be that bit higher. This, combined with being overweight and leading an unhealthy lifestyle, means the risk of hypertension is greatly increased. The Coronary Preven-tion Group would like all adults checked for high blood pressure every year.

FURTHER CAUSES

The following risk factors are all strongly linked with hypertension and are things that you can pay attention to and, there-fore, greatly increase your chances of leading a long and healthy life.

- *Smoking.* If anyone remains to be told — give it up!
- *Long-term stress.* We all have to cope with stressful situations from time to time which may result in temporary raised blood pressure. If this leads to continued worry and unrest, it can seriously affect some people's health and contribute to hypertension. As well

as finding ways of resolving or easing the stressful problems, ask your doctor about relaxation techniques. Also wherever possible avoid situations that cause you stress.

- *Lack of exercise.* Exercise taken regularly at your pace will help the heart work more efficiently and can help reduce hypertension. Moreover, the feeling of well-being and enjoyment derived from exercise will help to relieve stress. There's no need to take up an energetic sport or work-out at a gym every day, if that really doesn't appeal. Simply walking rather than using the car on short trips, or climbing the stairs rather than taking lifts or escalators will be beneficial.

- *Overweight.* Excess weight means that the heart has to pump harder and this puts up blood pressure. Keeping your weight down will help keep blood pressure down. (See chart on page 156 for recommended weights.)

- *Too much alcohol.* Blood-pressure rockets when you drink, so limit your consumption. The recommendations are not to drink more than 14 units a week for women, or 21 units for men. One unit is equivalent to a standard glass of wine or sherry, 300 ml/½ pint of beer, lager or cider or 1 pub measure of spirit. These are the upper limits. Naturally it's better to keep below them and not to drink alcohol every day of the week.

- *High salt intake.* The exact link between salt and high blood pressure is still not fully understood. Certainly we eat far more salt than we need or is good for us. A high salt intake can cause high blood pressure in people who are predisposed to this disorder and, for these people especially, reducing salt may well help to bring down raised blood pressure. The difficulty is, how do you know how susceptible you are? The simple answer is, you don't. It's impossible to single out individual causes when there are so many other possible factors. The sensible solution is for everyone to take what precautions they can, including eating less salt as part of their overall 'keeping healthy' plan. Certainly doctors recommend patients with hypertension to reduce their salt intake. This is discussed in further detail later.

- *Too much saturated fat.* An excess of fats, particularly the saturated type (generally animal fats which are hard at room temperature) leads to a build up of deposits in the arteries which again puts up blood pressure. Polyunsaturated fats, on the other hand, are generally believed to inhibit this clogging up process. More recently, monounsaturated fats (olive oil is high in this type of fatty acid), have been recognized as having a beneficial effect in fighting heart disease by helping to lower blood cholesterol. However, although it is advisable to switch to using the poly- and monounsaturated fats and oils, the overall recommendation is to reduce total fat. And, as far as weight control is concerned, don't be misled, they all have the same calorie value unless you choose a low-fat (or reduced-fat) spread.

PREVENTION AND TREATMENT — WHAT YOU CAN DO

As already discussed, there's a lot you can do by leading a healthier lifestyle. Taking more exercise, giving up smoking, watching your diet and losing some weight if you need to are all positively helpful. Your doctor may also prescribe pills if you are suffering from severe hypertension but the aim of this book is to help with diet, for this is the main area of prevention which you can very easily take responsibility for.

The Healthy Diet

SALT — HOW STRICT NEED YOU BE?

Contrary to general belief there is no need to cut out salt altogether from your diet. The Chest, Heart and Stroke Association recommend that it is advisable not to sprinkle additional salt over food at the table, but small amounts can be used in cooking. Doctors and dietitians advise reducing salt intake but not to the extent of making food unpalatable.

Some salt (sodium chloride) is essential to good health. It is necessary for the correct functioning of the kidneys and for maintaining the balance of body fluids. On average we eat between 10 and 14 grams of salt per day — equivalent to two whole teaspoons! If that surprises you, here's where it comes from:

- 50% of our salt intake comes in manufactured food
- 25% is added by us, in cooking and at table
- 25% occurs naturally in food

Most of us only need one to two grams of salt per day, although the requirement does increase in a hot climate, when salt is lost in sweat through the skin.

Removing the salt cellar from the table and cutting down on manufactured food are relatively painless ways of reducing your salt intake. Look at food labels when shopping and try to avoid those products which are high in salt. (See Shopping Sense.) Ingredients are always listed in order of the quantity in which they're used, so the higher up the list that salt comes, the more there is in the product.

When I first started this book, I tried not to use any ingredient which contained added salt. I would not consider myself to be a particularly salty person, but with tomato purée, curry paste, ready-mixed mustards and so many culinary flavourings 'banned', some of the resulting dishes were really rather bland. Of course, there's no need to go to this extreme. Simply note that when such ingredients are used in recipes, there's frequently no need for additional salt. Always taste first and ask yourself if any extra is really necessary. Herbs and spices, garlic, fresh ginger, fruit juices and so on can do wonders, as you'll discover.

Salt substitutes are useful for people who really are addicted to the flavour of salt and find it difficult to restrict its use in cooking or at the table. There are many proprietary brands available (based on potassium chloride) but they are not suitable for everyone so do check with your doctor first, before using. In fact, when you're making any dietary changes, it's always advisable to consult your doctor first. Salt restriction can be harmful for people with certain types of kidney disease so do not take any action without first seeking individual, personal advice.

CALCIUM IS ALSO IMPORTANT
Current research is investigating the role of calcium in the prevention of hypertension. Although no definite recommendations have emerged as yet, the importance of calcium in sustaining general good health, has been realized and an adequate intake is encouraged. Simply having 600 ml/1 pint of milk a day (skimmed or semi-skimmed, to reduce fat) will provide sufficient calcium. Yogurt and cheese (choose lower-fat varieties) are also good sources. Non-dairy foods containing calcium include canned fish, dark green vegetables, pulses, nuts and dried fruits. As with all nutrients, calcium should be provided by a variety of foods in a balanced diet. Apart from helping to prevent hypertension, an adequate intake of calcium is important for the growth of strong bones and teeth in children and helps protect against excessive bone loss (osteoporosis) in later life.

WEIGHT — THE SENSIBLE WAY TO DIET
As already discussed, being overweight is a serious risk factor so it's important to get your weight under control. There are all sorts of weight–loss diets but the sensible way is to stick to fresh wholefoods. Processed foods are nearly always high in fat and/or sugar and/or salt so should be avoided. Basically your diet should include plenty of fresh fruit and vegetables, lean

meat, fish and poultry, wholewheat cereals and pulses and low-fat dairy products. You need to cut out or at least restrict to occasional treats, chocolate, cream, hard fat and creamy cheese, fried foods, sugary foods and refined bakery items, such as cakes and biscuits.

Eating a wholefood diet will increase your intake of dietary fibre naturally — the main sources being wholewheat cereals, pulses, nuts, fresh and dried fruits and root and leafy vegetables. This increased bulk not only encourages a healthy digestion but considerably helps with dieting. High-fibre foods are very sustaining so your appetite is satisfied at meal times and the temptation to nibble between meals shouldn't arise. Snacks are usually high in fat and/or sugar and salt and are the enemy of weight watchers.

For fibre to work efficiently, it's important to include plenty of fluids in the diet. This should be between 1.1–1.75 litres/2–3 pints (2½–3¾ American pints) per day. Suitable drinks include tea and coffee (in moderation), unsweetened fruit juices, low-calorie squashes, milk (preferably skimmed or semi-skimmed) or, of course, water (bottled mineral or tap).

This is the healthiest way of losing weight, and you should find it relatively easy to stick to. It will also retrain your eating habits so you shouldn't put the weight you've lost back on again. I might add that this is not just advice for dieters,

but a style of eating which constitutes a healthy diet for everyone. The only difference for those trying to lose weight, rather than just maintain it, is that the choice and quantity of foods needs to be that bit stricter. For this reason, I have put calorie values on all the recipes to help. For an average weight loss of 1–1.5kg/2–3lb a week, women should aim for a daily intake of 1000–1200 Calories and men, around 1500 Calories.

SHOPPING SENSE
The general aim is to reduce fats (particularly the saturated type), sugar and salt and to increase fibre. These objectives will virtually take care of themselves if you choose fresh wholefoods and reduce manufactured and processed foods.

GO FOR:
- *Wholegrain cereals*, i.e., wholewheat pasta, brown rice, oats, wholewheat bread and so on. All are high in fibre, but remember that virtually all commercially made breakfast cereals contain added salt and sugar. Making your own muesli is a simple way of controlling these ingredients. There's a delicious recipe on page 25. Bread, too, contains salt, because a little is necessary for flavour. Unless your doctor has advised a completely salt-free regime, there's no need to stop buying bread. Few people have time to

make their own bread, but if you do, you can reduce the amount of salt in the recipe.

- *Pulses* (dried beans, peas and lentils). These, too, are an excellent source of fibre but buy the dried ones not the canned variety which will be high in salt. Dried are more economical, too, but will require soaking and longer cooking.
- *Plenty of fresh fruit and vegetables.* If you do buy canned products, choose fruits in natural fruit juice and not syrup. Canned vegetables and beans are nearly always in brine or salt solutions, although a few manufacturers are beginning to produce canned vegetables without added salt. Always read the label and preferably choose the fresh variety.
- *Skimmed or semi-skimmed milk.* Semi-skimmed (low fat) has only half the fat of whole milk and skimmed has almost no fat at all. So, as well as being healthier, they help considerably with a weight–loss programme. If you have a number of hot drinks throughout the day and use a fair amount of milk in cooking, the calorie saving will be quite significant.
- *Polyunsaturated or monosaturated fats and oils.* This includes sunflower, safflower, corn, soya, grapeseed, olive and nut oils and magarines labelled high in polyunsaturates. They are no lower in

calories, but are healthier in helping to prevent heart disease. You can also now buy low-salt polyunsaturated margarines, which are a good choice. On occasions you can use unsalted butter, but generally it's better to choose a polyunsaturated fat than butter of any sort, which will always be high in saturated fat.

- *Fish (apart from smoked fish which is high in salt) and poultry.* These are both lower in fat than red meat but poultry should always be skinned. Don't buy prepared products which have been crumbed or battered.
- *Lean meat and game.* Animals are now bred to be very much leaner and supermarkets have come a long way in promoting leaner cuts. It's always worth paying a little more than buying a cheaper, fattier cut. A butcher will always mince a piece of lean meat for you if you're unsure of the fat content of ready-prepared mince. Game, such as venison and pheasant, contains little fat and is becoming much more readily available in season.

AVOID:
- *Canned and processed meats.* This includes salami, sausages, hamburgers, pâtés, pies, corned beef and so on. They are all high in salt and fat.
- *Smoked fish* is dipped in brine before being smoked so has a high salt

content. It's therefore wise to only have it occasionally, unless of course your doctor has advised it being completely omitted.

- *Canned fish*, too, such as tuna, is frequently packed in brine. Even those canned in oil have salt added. These should therefore only be eaten occasionally and, as with any food, always try to choose the fresh alternative.
- *Bacon, ham and cheese* are all quite high in salt, as it's partly used for preserving as well as to improve texture and flavour. It's better to use a small amount of a mature flavoured cheese than a large amount of a mild one. This will also help reduce fat and calories. As with smoked fish, you can eat them occasionally. If your consumption of these foods has been high, it is advisable to cut back.
- *Butter, lard, block margarines, shortenings and drippings*. All these are high in saturated fat.
- *Cream.* Choose lower-fat varieties or yogurt.
- *Mayonnaise, salad cream and salad dressings*. Commercial varieties always contain salt, so it's better to make your own salad dressings at home. If you use commercial varieties, at least go for those which are labelled 'high in polyunsaturates' or, if you're dieting, the reduced-calorie varieties.
- *Pickles, sauces, relishes* rely heavily on salt and sugar for flavour.
- *Canned and packet soups* are high in salt. Homemade soup doesn't take long to make and it freezes well.
- *Manufactured cakes, biscuits, pastries and puddings*. These are high in saturated fats, sugar, salt and calories. If you're having three good meals a day, these foods are unnecessary, and will only help contribute to health and weight problems.
- *Salted nuts and crisps*. These, of course, are high in salt and fat. Choose unsalted nuts or fruit instead, although weight–watchers should take note of the high calorie value of nuts and dried fruits. It's all right to use them in cooking but nibbled between meals, the calories will mount up.
- *Sugary drinks*. These are high in calories. It's always better to have fresh fruit juices, sugar–free drinks or mineral water.

COOKING WITH CARE
- Use herbs and spices for flavouring in place of salt. Cook without salt — then taste and only add a little if the flavour really is unpalatable. If you're used to always salting your food in the past, begin by cutting down gradually. And remember that many flavourings, such as tomato purée (paste) and made-up mustards, contain salt already, so additional salt may well be unnecessary.

- Stock cubes may be used but they are relatively high in salt. Try using just half a cube or, better still, make your own stock whenever there's time. (See recipes on pages 29–30 for chicken and vegetable stock.)
- Trim excess fat off meat and remove skin from poultry before cooking.
- When making meat dishes, use a little less meat and bulk up the quantity with pulses or vegetables.
- Always grill rather than fry. When frying is necessary, use a non-stick pan which will enable you to use less fat. Strain off any excess fat after frying and drain food on absorbent kitchen paper.
- Roast meat on a rack so that the fat drips through underneath.
- Use low-fat natural (plain) yogurt in place of cream in cooking. If it's to be heated, stabilize the yogurt first by blending a little cornflour into the yogurt (1 teaspoon to 150ml/¼ pint). Low-fat cream substitutes can also be used.

ABOUT THE RECIPES

As stressed at the beginning, these recipes, and the healthy eating principles behind them, are not only for people suffering from high blood pressure but for anyone wanting to do all they can to stay healthy. Also, if someone in the family has hypertension, it's not only easier but advisable for all the family to follow the same diet.

The diet is for children as well as adults, and remember that good habits learnt at an early age will establish a healthy pattern for a lifetime. The recipes are intended to be quick and simple, using readily-available ingredients you can find in most large supermarkets. Occasionally you may need to pop into a health food shop or an ethnic store for something slightly more unusual, but the general aim is that shopping should not pose a problem.

In the main, the recipes follow the recommended healthy eating principles, to reduce fat (particularly the saturated type), reduce sugar, reduce salt and increase fibre. I say in the main, because occasionally I've used basmati rice rather than brown, because I don't believe in spoiling the recipe for the sake of, in this case, a little extra fibre. It's the total diet which matters and as long as the above guidelines are generally heeded, there's no need to go to extremes.

Many of the recipes are simply well-known or classic dishes, adapted to be healthier. Others are personal favourites, many from other countries which can teach us a lot about alternative flavourings. By using herbs, spices and flower waters, salt can frequently be omitted altogether.

In many recipes I've stated stock or water. This really depends on how strict a low-salt diet your doctor recommends. As mentioned before, most people needn't make strict limitations. Personally, I found that in most recipes, other flavourings more than made up for a lack of salt. I haven't specified salt-free tomato purées (pastes) and so on, because although these can be found, they are not readily available.

I have included calorie values on all the recipes because I believe this to be helpful and to have some constructive meaning. Dividing the meal you cook by six instead of four portions will, of course, decrease the calorific value per portion, as the relevant recipes show.

The desserts are largely based on fruit with fruit juices frequently used to sweeten. Consequently, none is high calorie. Where it was necessary to use some added sugar, weight-watchers can reduce calories further by substituting an artificial sweetener.

I've purposely not included salt content analyses because a doctor will rarely tell you what salt intake to aim for. The suggested figure is to reduce intake to around 5 grams (5,000 milligrams) a day. But to put a lot of figures on a recipe, I feel, is largely meaningless and frequently confusing. Does anyone really want to sit down and analyse everything they eat? Eating should be about pleasure and enjoyment. If you're eating a fresh, wholefood diet, reducing manufactured and processed foods and cutting out salt at the table and much of it in cooking, you're making a very significant change for the better. Put that together with all the other lifestyle recommendations, and you stand a good chance of leading a long and healthy life.

BREAKFASTS

Strawberry and Banana Yogurt Shake

Really fast for mornings when you're pushed for time. Other fruit yogurts can be substituted with a matching flavour jam.

Serves 2
200 Calories a glass

UK

1 large banana
150ml/¼ pint low fat strawberry yogurt
1 tablespoon reduced-sugar strawberry
   jam
450ml/¾ pint skimmed milk, chilled

US

1 large banana
⅔ cup low-fat strawberry yogurt
1 tablespoon reduced-sugar strawberry
   jam
2 cups skimmed milk, chilled

1. Slice the banana and place in a blender or food processor with the rest of the ingredients. Mix together, then pour into 2 tall glasses.

Not suitable for freezing.

Wake-Up Bowl

Lots of colourful fresh fruit to give an energizing start to the day. You can use any variety of grapefruit, such as the pink-fleshed Ruby Red or the even sweeter Sunrise grapefruit which have a deep red flesh.

Serves 2
95 Calories a portion

UK	**US**
1 grapefruit	1 grapefruit
1 orange	1 orange
1 kiwi fruit	1 kiwi fruit
1 passion fruit	1 passion fruit
125ml/4 fl oz cranberry juice	½ cup cranberry juice

1. Cut away the peel and pith from the grapefruit and orange. Cut flesh into segments over a bowl to catch the juice.
2. Peel the kiwi fruit, cut into wedges and add to the bowl.
3. Cut passion fruit in half and scoop the pulpy centre into a jug. Top with cranberry juice and pour over the fruit.

Not suitable for freezing.

Banana, Date and Walnut Yogurt⎯⎯⎯⎯

A delicious, high-fibre combination of fresh and dried fruit with the nutty crunch of walnuts. It's best to mix the chopped dates into the yogurt and leave overnight to soften.

Serves 4
225 Calories a portion

UK

100g/4 oz dried, stoned dates
300ml/½ pint natural low-fat yogurt
2 bananas
50g/2 oz walnut pieces

US

⅔ cup dried, stoned dates
1¼ cups plain, low-fat yogurt
2 bananas
½ cup walnuts

1. Chop dates and stir into yogurt in a bowl. Cover and leave overnight.
2. Slice and fold in the bananas.
3. Roughly chop walnuts and scatter over the top.

Not suitable for freezing.

Prune and Orange Compote

Use the no-need-to-soak dried prunes. All they require is a very brief cooking in some fruit juice to plump them up.

Serves 4
160 Calories a portion (without yogurt and nuts)

UK

225g/8 oz dried, stoned prunes
300ml/½ pint unsweetened pineapple (or other fruit) juice
2–3 juicy oranges
low-fat natural yogurt (optional)
chopped hazelnuts (optional)

US

1⅓ cups dried, stoned prunes
1⅓ cups unsweetened pineapple (or other fruit) juice
2–3 juicy oranges
low-fat plain yogurt (optional)
chopped hazelnuts (optional)

1. Place prunes in a small pan with the juice. Bring to the boil, cover and simmer for 5 minutes. Then take off heat and allow to cool.
2. Cut away skin and pith from oranges, then cut fruit, between the membranes, into neat segments catching the juice in a bowl.
3. Stir oranges and any juice into prunes. Chill.
4. Serve, if liked, with yogurt and sprinkle with hazlenuts.

Not suitable for freezing.

Fruity Porridge

Porridge is an ideal breakfast dish, especially on a cold morning. It's warming and sustaining and takes very little time to prepare. For a change try making porridge with diluted fruit juice instead of milk or water. Quantities can be easily increased to serve any number of people.

Serves 1 (generous portion)
340 Calories

UK

(40g) 1½ oz porridge oats
(250ml) 8 fl oz unsweetened apple or
   orange juice
(25g) 1 oz raisins, sultanas or dried
   apricots
125ml/4 fl oz water
low-fat natural yogurt (optional)

US

½ cup rolled oats
1 cup unsweetened apple or orange juice
2 tablespoons raisins or dried apricots
½ cup water
low-fat plain yogurt (optional)

1. Put oats, juice and your choice of dried fruit together in a pan and add the water. If you wish, you can use less juice and make up the quantity with more water.
2. Bring to the boil, then simmer for 2–3 minutes, stirring occasionally, until thickened.
3. Serve topped with yogurt, if liked.

Not suitable for freezing.

Peanut and Raisin Granola

This is a crunchy American-style cereal, rather like toasted muesli. It's worth making up a large quantity since the dry mix will store well in an airtight container. Serve with skimmed milk, yogurt or juice poured over. If liked, top with fresh fruit, such as sliced peaches.

Serves 8
415 Calories a portion

UK

225g/8 oz porridge oats
50g/2 oz wheatgerm
75g/3 oz unsalted peanuts (or almonds or cashews)
50g/2 oz sunflower seeds
50g/2 oz sesame seeds
1 teaspoon ground cinnamon
4 tablespoons sunflower oil
4 tablespoons clear honey
150ml/¼ pint unsweetened apple juice
100g/4 oz raisins

US

2½ cups rolled oats
½ cup wheatgerm
⅔ cup unsalted peanuts (or almonds or cashews)
⅓ cup sunflower seeds
⅓ cup sesame seeds
1 teaspoon ground cinnamon
5 tablespoons sunflower oil
5 tablespoons clear honey
⅔ cup unsweetened apple juice
⅔ cup raisins

1. Combine the oats, wheatgerm, nuts, seeds and cinnamon in a large bowl.
2. Blend together the oil, honey and apple juice. Pour into the oat mixture and mix well.
3. Spread mixture in a roasting tin (baking pan) and cook at 150°C/300°F gas mark 2 for about 30 minutes, turning over the top layer from time to time so that the mixture browns and crisps evenly all over.
4. Stir in raisins. Allow to cool, then store in airtight container.

Tropical Muesli

Homemade muesli is unbeatable. Simply start with a base of oats, then add any variety of nuts, seeds and dried fruits you fancy. This version has a tropical flavour, containing dried banana, pineapple and coconut. Serve with skimmed milk and top with any fresh seasonal fruit, such as apples, peaches or bananas but when available, soft fruits are the most delicious addition.

Serves 8
240 Calories a portion

UK

100g/ 4 oz jumbo oats
75g/3 oz toasted wheatflakes
50g/2 oz hazelnuts or walnuts
50g/2 oz dried apricots
25g/1 oz dried pineapple pieces
25g/1 oz dried banana chips
15g/½ oz unsweetened coconut flakes
50g /2 oz raisins or sultanas
25g/1 oz pumpkin seeds
25g/1 oz sunflower seeds

US

1¼ cups rolled oats
2 cups wholewheat breakfast flakes
½ cup hazelnuts or walnuts
⅓ cup dried apricots
¼ cup dried pineapple pieces
¼ cup dried banana chips
⅙ cup unsweetened coconut flakes
⅓ cup raisins
¼ cup pumpkin seeds
¼ cup sunflower seeds

1. Stir together the oats and wheatflakes (breakfast flakes) in a large bowl.
2. Chop nuts, apricots and any large pieces of pineapple and banana into small pieces. Mix all the ingredients into the oats.
3. Store in an airtight container. It will keep fresh for several weeks.

Apple and Raisin Pancakes

Pancakes make an unusual breakfast. They can be prepared in advance and take very little time to assemble just before eating. They are very versatile and can be filled with different kinds of fruit or savoury mixtures. Serve these for a weekend breakfast treat or a late morning Brunch.

Makes 12
110 Calories each

UK

BATTER:

100g/4 oz wholewheat flour
300 ml/½ pint skimmed milk
1 egg
1 tablespoon sunflower oil

FILLING:

675g/1½ lb cooking apples
25g/1 oz polyunsaturated margarine
75g/3 oz raisins
½ teaspoon mixed spice

US

BATTER:

1 cup wholewheat flour
1¼ cups skim milk
1 egg
1 tablespoon sunflower oil

FILLING:

1½ pounds cooking apples
2½ tablespoons polyunsaturated margarine
½ cup raisins
½ teaspoon mixed spice

1. First make the batter. Place flour in a bowl, make a well in the centre and add a little of the milk, the egg and the oil. Whisk the flour into the liquid, then gradually blend in the rest of the milk, keeping the batter smooth and free from lumps. (If using a food processor or blender, simply put in the milk, egg and oil, spoon the flour on top then blend for just a few seconds. Use the metal blade on a processor.) The batter is best left for about 30 minutes to allow time for the starch cells to swell, giving lighter pancakes.

2. For the filling, peel, core and slice the apples and place in a heavy-based pan with the margarine and 2 tablespoons water. Cook gently until the apples begin to soften, then add the raisins and spice. Continue cooking until soft but not mushy.

3. Lightly grease a pancake pan or a non-stick frying pan (skillet) with just a smear of

oil. Pour in about 2 tablespoons of the batter, swirl it around to cover the base of the pan and cook for about 1 minute until set and lightly browned on the underside. Flip over and cook the other side for about 30 seconds. Tip onto a heated plate and keep warm. Cook remaining pancakes in the same way, lightly greasing the pan between pancakes.

4. Fill pancakes with apple mixture, roll up and serve with natural (plain) yogurt if liked.

COOK'S NOTE: To make in advance, stack pancakes interleaved with kitchen paper or greaseproof (baking parchment). Keep in the refrigerator. To reheat, cover stack with foil and place over a pan of hot water. To reheat in the microwave, place 4 pancakes at a time on a piece of kitchen paper and cook on Full Power for 1 minute.

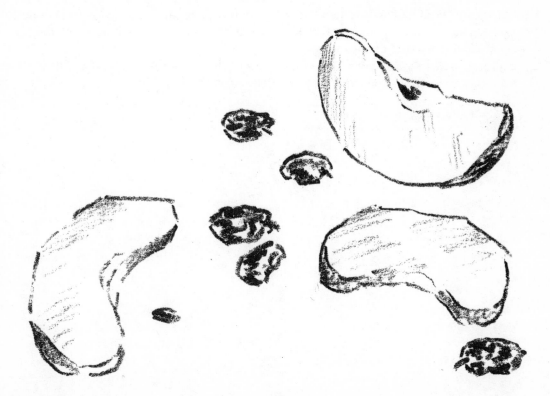

Fresh Grapefruit and Strawberry Shells___

Colourful and refreshing. Pink-fleshed Ruby Red grapefruit are sweeter tasting than the regular yellow-skinned ones also known as white grapefruit. Something unusual to look out for are Sweeties — large green-skinned seedless grapefruit which are deliciously sweet. If strawberries are expensive, use fewer and add 1 peeled and sliced orange.

Serves 2
40 Calories a portion

UK	**US**
1 grapefruit	1 grapefruit
175g/6 oz fresh strawberries	1 cup fresh strawberries

1. Cut grapefruit in half and using a curved grapefruit knife or a serrated knife, cut out flesh as neatly as you can between the membranes. Scrape out any remaining membrane to leave 2 clean shells.
2. Hull and halve strawberries and combine with the grapefruit segments. Pile fruit back into grapefruit shells and serve chilled.

Not suitable for freezing.

SOUPS AND STARTERS

STOCKS

Many of the recipes in this book have stock as one of the ingredients. Commercially-made stock cubes are rather salty so, to lessen the salt content, use half the stock cube to the same quantity of water. However, it is better to use home-made stock, which will have a better flavour and need not have salt added to it. Stock takes very little time and effort to make, as you'll see below.

Chicken Stock

Chicken giblets and carcass
1 large carrot or carrot peelings
2 sticks celery
½ onion, stuck with 4 cloves
strip of lemon peel
2 bay leaves
bunch of parsley stalks
2 sprigs of fresh thyme and/or sage
few black peppercorns

1. Break up carcass, removing any skin. Chop carrots and celery. Place all the ingredients in a large pan, cover with cold water, then bring to the boil. Turn down heat, cover and simmer for about 1 hour.
2. Strain, discard the flavourings and leave stock to cool. Chill in the refrigerator. Any fat present will settle on the surface and can be easily skimmed off before the stock is used. Use within 2 days or freeze.

Use within 6 months if frozen.
Reheat from frozen or thaw overnight in the refrigerator.

Vegetable Stock

There is no doubt that making soup with stock rather than water adds extra flavour. You can use the trimmings from prepared vegetables, so nothing is wasted. It's best to avoid green vegetables such as cabbage, broccoli or Brussels sprouts as they can give stock rather too strong a flavour.

You will need:

root vegetable peelings, such as carrot,
   parsnip and potato
1 large leek or onion
2 bay leaves
bunch of parsley stalks
few sprigs of thyme
any other fresh herbs, such as tarragon,
   sage or rosemary
6–8 black peppercorns

1. Chop all the trimmings and any vegetables you're using and place in a large pan. Cover with cold water and bring to the boil. Turn down heat, cover and simmer for about 1 hour.
2. Strain, discard flavourings and leave stock to cool. Chill and use within 2 days or freeze.

Use within 6 months if frozen.
Reheat from frozen or thaw overnight in the refrigerator.

Curried Parsnip and Apple Soup

Parsnips have a very distinctive flavour which people tend to love or hate. For those who are fond of the flavour, they make an excellent winter soup. The spices in the curry paste harmonize wonderfully with the sweetness of the parsnips.

Serves 4–6
190–130 Calories a portion

UK

675g/1½ lb parsnips
2 leeks
1 large cooking apple
25g/1 oz polyunsaturated margarine
2 teaspoons mild curry paste
1.1 litres/2 pints vegetable stock or water
freshly ground black pepper
shredded leek, to garnish

US

1½ pounds parsnips
2 leeks
1 large cooking apple
2½ tablespoons polyunsaturated margarine
2 teaspoons mild curry paste
5 cups vegetable stock or water
freshly ground black pepper
shredded leek, to garnish

1. Peel and chop parsnips. Slice and wash leeks. Peel, core and chop apple.
2. Melt margarine gently in a large non-stick saucepan, add the parsnips, leeks and apple and sweat gently for about 5 minutes.
3. Stir in the curry paste, cook for 1 minute, then pour in the stock. Bring to the boil, then simmer gently for 30 minutes or until the parsnips are tender.
4. Using a draining spoon, lift out the vegetables into a food processor or blender and blend to a smooth purée.
5. Return purée to liquid in pan, reheat and season to taste with pepper. Serve garnished with shredded leek.

Suitable for freezing. Use within 3 months
Reheat gently from frozen.

Goulash and Red Pepper Soup

A hearty, main-meal soup. Be sure to use a good-quality lean beef, not an economy mince (ground beef) which will have a higher proportion of fat. Supermarkets frequently label their premium mince 'extra lean' or you can always ask your butcher to mince a lean cut for you.

Serves 4
280 Calories a portion

UK

2 onions
1 clove garlic
(450g) 1 lb lean minced beef
3 tomatoes
1 red pepper
2 medium potatoes
(600ml) 1 pint stock
2 teaspoons sherry vinegar or red wine vinegar
1 tablespoon tomato purée
1 tablespoon paprika
2 teaspoons sugar
1 bouquet garni
2 teaspoons cornflour

US

2 onions
1 clove garlic
1 pound lean ground beef
3 tomatoes
1 red bell pepper
2 medium potatoes
2½ cups stock
2 teaspoons sherry vinegar or red wine vinegar
1 tablespoon tomato paste
1 tablespoon paprika
2 teaspoons sugar
1 bouquet garni
2 teaspoons cornstarch

1. Peel and roughly slice the onions and crush the garlic.
2. Place the beef in a non-stick saucepan and brown gently — there's no need to add any fat, even lean mince contains sufficient fat to prevent it sticking. Once the meat starts to brown, add the onions and garlic and continue cooking until the onions are soft.
3. Chop the tomatoes, cut the pepper into large dice, removing the seeds and peel and cube the potatoes. Add to the pan together with the stock, vinegar, purée (paste), paprika, sugar and bouquet garni. Bring to the boil, then cover and simmer for about 20 minutes until the potatoes are tender.

4. Blend the cornflour (cornstarch) with a little water and stir into the soup to thicken. Remove bouquet garni and check seasoning.

May be frozen. Use within 3 months.
Reheat gently from frozen.

COOK'S NOTE: A bouquet garni is made up from bay leaf, thyme and parsley tied in a small piece of muslin. A little marjoram, oregano or basil can also be added.

Tomato, Apple and Celery Soup

I always think soups taste so much more interesting when made with a mix of ingredients although you do need to watch that your flavours harmonize. Here's a favourite of mine for late summer.

Serves 4
150 Calories a portion

UK

1 medium onion
3 sticks celery
5 large flavourful tomatoes
2 dessert apples
25g/1 oz polyunsaturated margarine
1 tablespoon sunflower oil
600ml/1 pint vegetable stock
1 tablespoon tomato purée
1 tablespoon sherry (optional)
1 teaspoon sugar
½ teaspoon dried basil
freshly ground black pepper
celery leaves to garnish

US

1 medium onion
3 celery stalks
5 large flavorful tomatoes
2 dessert apples
2½ tablespoons polyunsaturated
  margarine
1 tablespoon sunflower oil
2½ cups vegetable stock
1 tablespoon tomato paste
1 tablespoon sherry (optional)
1 teaspoon sugar
½ teaspoon dried basil
freshly ground black pepper
celery leaves to garnish

1. Roughly chop the onion, celery, tomatoes and apples, removing the apple cores. It's unnecessary to peel the apples and skin the tomatoes as the soup will be liquidized before serving. As well as saving time on peeling, the skins will help add colour and flavour to the soup.
2. Heat the margarine and the oil in a large saucepan, add the onion and celery and sweat for about 5 minutes until the onion is golden.
3. Add the tomatoes and apples to the pan, stir around, then pour in the stock. Add tomato purée (paste), the sherry, which adds considerably to the flavour, sugar, basil and plenty of pepper. Bring to the boil, then cover and simmer gently for about 15 minutes.

4. Tip soup into a food processor or blender (you may need to do this in two batches to avoid over-filling the container) and liquidize until smooth. Tip back into pan, check seasoning and heat through. Serve garnished with celery leaves.

May be frozen. Use within 3 months.
Reheat gently from frozen.

Sprout and Almond Soup

This uses a rather unusual combination of Brussels sprouts and almonds, and it's absolutely delicious. I also find that young people, who can be very fussy about eating vegetables, enjoy it very much.

Serves 4–6
275–185 Calories a portion

UK	**US**
1 large onion	1 large onion
450g/1 lb Brussels sprouts	1 pound Brussels sprouts
50g/2 oz polyunsaturated margarine	¼ cup polyunsaturated margarine
75g/3 oz blanched almonds	⅔ cup blanched almonds
1.1 litres/2 pints vegetable stock	5 cups vegetable stock
1 bouquet garni (see note p.33)	1 bouquet garni (see note p.33)
freshly grated nutmeg	freshly grated nutmeg
freshly ground black pepper	freshly ground black pepper
chives or parsley, to garnish	chives or parsley, to garnish

1. Chop the onion and trim the sprouts.
2. Melt the margarine in a pan and gently cook the onion and almonds until the nuts are golden. Then stir in the sprouts.
3. Pour in stock, add the bouquet garni, cover and cook gently for 10–15 minutes until the sprouts are tender.
4. Using a draining spoon, lift out the sprouts, nuts and onions into a blender or food processor and blend to a smooth purée. Return purée to liquid in the pan, stirring it in.
5. Season to taste with nutmeg and pepper. Heat through gently.
6. Snip some chives or parsley over the top to serve.

May be frozen. Use within 3 months.
Thaw overnight in the refrigerator, then reheat gently

COOK'S NOTE: You can add extra flavour by seasoning with onion and herb peppers.

Garlicky Potato, Leek and Watercress Soup

This is always popular and the addition of watercress as an integral ingredient adds flavour and colour to the soup.

Serves 4-6
240-160 Calories a portion

UK	**US**
2 leeks	2 leeks
450g/1 lb potatoes	1 pound potatoes
50g/2 oz polyunsaturated margarine	¼ cup polyunsaturated margarine
3 cloves garlic	3 cloves garlic
225g/8 oz watercress	4 cups watercress
750ml/1¼ pints vegetable stock	3 cups vegetable stock
1 bay leaf	1 bay leaf
freshly ground black pepper	freshly ground black pepper
small bunch of parsley	small bunch of parsley

1. Trim and slice leeks. Scrub and cube potatoes.
2. Heat margarine in a heavy-based pan and sweat the leeks and potatoes until the leeks are soft.
3. Crush garlic and stir in. Trim watercress and stir in. Cook gently for a couple of minutes until the watercress has just wilted.
4. Pour in stock, add bay leaf and season with pepper. Cover and cook gently for 15-20 minutes until the potatoes are tender.
5. Using a draining spoon, lift out the vegetables into a blender or food processor and purée until smooth. Return to pan and stir into liquid. Reheat and add more pepper if needed.
6. Finely chop a couple of tablespoons of parsley and stir in.

> May be frozen. Use within 3 months.
> Thaw overnight in the refrigerator then reheat gently.

Milanese Vegetable Soup

A very substantial meal-in-itself soup, packed with vegetables, beans and rice. Vegetarians can omit the bacon. It can be served sprinkled with a little freshly grated Parmesan cheese. Note that you need to soak the dried beans overnight before making the soup.

Serves 4-6
300-200 Calories a portion

UK

100g/4 oz dried borlotti or red kidney
  beans
2 rashers lean bacon
2 sticks celery
1 onion
1-2 cloves garlic
450g/1 lb tomatoes
1-2 tablespoons olive oil
1.4 litres/2½ pints vegetable stock
1 teaspoon dried basil
freshly ground black pepper
50g/2 oz brown rice
4 carrots
225g/8 oz cabbage (or courgettes, green
  beans or peas)

US

½ cup dried borlotti or red kidney beans
2 slices back bacon
2 celery stalks
1 onion
1-2 cloves garlic
1 pound tomatoes
1-2 tablespoons olive oil
6¼ cups vegetable stock
1 teaspoon dried basil
freshly ground black pepper
½ cup brown rice
4 carrots
2 cups cabbage (or zucchini, snap beans
  or peas)

1. Soak the dried beans overnight in cold water. (If using dried kidney beans they then need to be boiled rapidly in fresh water for 10 minutes to destroy any toxins, before continuing with the recipe.)
2. Remove rind and any excess fat from bacon, then cut into small pieces. Chop celery and onion, crush garlic and skin and chop tomatoes.
3. Heat oil in a large saucepan, add the bacon (if using), celery, onion and garlic and sauté gently for about 5 minutes.

4. Stir in the tomatoes and the drained beans, pour in the stock, add basil and season with pepper. Bring to the boil, cover and cook gently for 1 hour, until the beans are tender.
5. Add rice and cook for a further 20 minutes.
6. Meanwhile, peel and slice carrots and finely shred cabbage. If you are using other vegetables, dice courgettes (zucchini) and cut beans in half or quarters.
7. Add remaining vegetables and cook for a further 10–15 minutes until the rice and vegetables are tender. Top up with more water or stock if necessary, although the consistency should be more like a stew than a soup. Add more pepper if needed.

May be frozen. Use within 1 month.
Thaw overnight in the refrigerator then reheat gently.

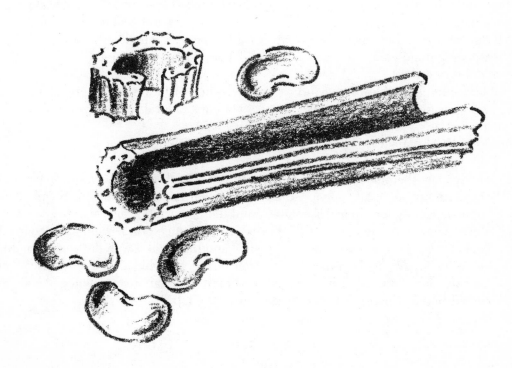

Spicy Peanut Dip

So many dips are either cheese- or mayonnaise-based and, therefore, quite salty. Here's one using unsalted peanuts which is similar to Indonesian satay sauce. Serve this dip with raw vegetable crudités.

Serves 6–8
210–160 Calories a portion

UK

1 large onion
1 tablespoon sunflower oil
2 cloves garlic
small piece fresh root ginger
2 teaspoons ground coriander
1 teaspoon ground cumin
pinch of turmeric
300ml/½ pint natural low-fat yogurt
175g/6 oz natural roasted peanuts
1 lemon
small bunch of parsley

US

1 large onion
1 tablespoon sunflower oil
2 cloves garlic
small piece fresh root ginger
2 teaspoons ground coriander
1 teaspoon ground cumin
pinch of turmeric
1¼ cups plain low-fat yogurt
1⅓ cups natural roasted peanuts
1 lemon
small bunch of parsley

1. Finely chop the onion, then fry in oil until soft. Crush garlic, peel and finely chop ginger and stir both into onion and fry for a further minute. Stir in spices and yogurt and cook gently for about 15 minutes until the mixture thickens slightly.
2. Meanwhile, place the nuts in a food processor or coffee grinder and chop coarsely.
3. Grate the lemon rind and squeeze the juice and then add it with the yogurt mixture to the nuts, still in the processor or transferred to a blender. Blend everything together — the dip won't be completely smooth, but with a consistency like sloppy peanut butter. Chop parsley and scatter over the top.

Not suitable for freezing.

SHOPPING NOTE: Natural roasted peanuts are roasted without oils, fats or salt; dry roasted peanuts are salted. You can use regular unsalted peanuts, but you will need to skin them first. Place under the grill for a few minutes, then tip on a clean tea towel, and lightly crush with a rolling pin to remove skins. Place back under grill to roast, for extra flavour.

Aubergine Caviar

I first tasted this delicious dip at an Egyptian tent lunch, while holidaying in Cairo. It makes an excellent starter served with some raw vegetable crudités and warm wholemeal pitta bread, or a simple meal spooned on baked jacket potatoes with a dollop of natural (plain) yogurt.

Serves 4–8
85–45 Calories a portion

UK

3 aubergines
1–2 cloves garlic
1 lemon
fresh parsley
2 tablespoons olive oil
1 teaspoon sesame oil (optional)
freshly ground black pepper

US

3 eggplants
1–2 cloves garlic
1 lemon
fresh parsley
2–3 tablespoons olive oil
1 teaspoon sesame oil (optional)
freshly ground black pepper

1. Bake the aubergines (eggplants) in the oven at 220°C/425°F Gas Mark 7 for about 30 minutes, until black on the outside. Then carefully peel off the skin, holding the aubergines under running cold water.
2. Place aubergine flesh in a sieve (wire mesh colander) and press down with a spoon to remove the excess juice, since it's rather bitter.
3. Then tip the flesh into a food processor or blender. Crush garlic, squeeze lemon juice and finely chop about 3 tablespoons parsley. Add all these to the aubergine. Gradually pour in the oil and blend everything together. (The oil can be poured down the feed tube of a processor while it's blending.) Add sesame oil, if using. Season to taste with pepper.

Not suitable for freezing.

Guacamole

A popular Mexican dip using avocado. There are many variations, some mild, others quite fiery. If you like it hot, simply add a couple of chopped, deseeded green chillies. A wonderful addition is chopped fresh coriander (cilantro) which you can get from some supermarkets or greengrocers. As well as serving as a dip, Guacamole makes a nice filling for scooped out tomatoes, or it can be spooned onto baked jacket potatoes or spread on wholewheat bread to make a delicious sandwich.

Serves 6
115 Calories a portion

UK	**US**
½ small onion	½ small onion
2 ripe avocados	2 ripe avocados
1 lemon	1 lemon
1 fat clove garlic	1 fat clove garlic
3–4 tomatoes	3–4 tomatoes
½ green pepper	½ green bell pepper
freshly ground black pepper	freshly ground black pepper

1. Chop the onion very finely and place in a bowl. Halve avocados, remove stone and scoop flesh into bowl. Squeeze juice from lemon, crush garlic and add both to the avocado. Mash with a fork and blend together until smooth. (This can be done in a food processor.)
2. Pour boiling water onto tomatoes in a bowl. Leave for 30 seconds, then drain and cover with cold water. This will loosen the skins which can then be peeled off. Chop and deseed tomatoes.
3. Finely chop and deseed pepper. Stir tomatoes and peppers into avocado mixture and season with pepper. Cover and keep chilled. Serve within a few hours of making before the avocado discolours.

Not suitable for freezing.

Cucumber Yogurt with Walnuts and Coriander

This makes a very tasty dip, which is especially good with crunchy vegetables. It can also be used as a topping for baked jacket potatoes or as a side dish to anything cooked with spices.

Serves 6   80 Calories a portion

UK

⅓ cucumber
50g/2 oz walnuts or natural roasted
    peanuts
small bunch of fresh coriander
300ml/½ pint natural low-fat yogurt
1 tablespoon cumin seeds
a little cayenne pepper

US

⅓ cucumber
½ cup walnuts or natural roasted peanuts
small bunch of fresh cilantro
1¼ cups plain low-fat yogurt
1 tablespoon cumin seeds
a little cayenne pepper

1. Dice cucumber. Roughly chop walnuts. Finely chop 1 tablespoon of coriander (cilantro).
2. Place cumin seeds in a small frying pan (skillet), without any oil, and heat for a few minutes until they look toasted. This brings out their flavour.
3. Pour yogurt into a serving dish and stir in coriander (cilantro), cucumber, walnuts and cumin seeds. Sprinkle with a little cayenne pepper. Serve chilled.

Not suitable for freezing.

Mixed Vegetable Brochettes

Vegetables marinated in a herb–and–garlic marinade and prepared on bamboo skewers make a colourful starter. Alternatively, they can be quickly grilled to make an easy light meal served with some rice. The same marinade can be used for prawns or cubes of lean lamb or poultry.

Serves 4   170 Calories a portion

UK

4 tablespoons olive oil
2 tablespoons lemon or lime juice
1 teaspoon wholegrain mustard
1 fat clove garlic
small bunch parsley
freshly ground black pepper
selection of fresh vegetables such as
   peppers, mushrooms, cherry tomatoes,
   baby sweetcorn, courgettes, onions

US

5 tablespoons olive oil
2 tablespoons lemon or lime juice
1 teaspoon wholegrain mustard
1 fat clove garlic
small bunch parsley
freshly ground black pepper
selection of fresh vegetables such as bell
   peppers, mushrooms, cherry tomatoes,
   baby sweetcorn, zucchini, onions

1. Mix together the oil, lemon or lime juice and mustard in a large shallow dish. Crush in the garlic. Finely chop about 2 tablespoons parsley and stir in to the marinade and season with pepper.
2. Cut vegetables into neat bite-sized pieces — mushrooms and tomatoes can be left whole unless quite large, in which case they should be halved. Aim to have all the vegetables much the same size.
3. Stir vegetables into marinade, turning them over several times then cover and leave for several hours.
4. Thread onto small skewers, preferably bamboo ones. If you use bamboo skewers, soak then for about 10 minutes in water to prevent them burning under the grill.
5. Grill brochettes for about 10 minutes, turning them occasionally until the vegetables are beginning to brown. Serve immediately with any remaining marinade spooned over.

Not suitable for freezing.

Stuffed Avocado Salad

Grapefruit, tuna and watercress folded into natural (plain) yogurt makes a refreshing combination to pile into creamy-fleshed avocados.

Serves 4
295 Calories a portion

UK

5 tablespoons natural low-fat yogurt
1 grapefruit
100g/3½ oz can tuna
1 bunch of watercress
2 avocados

US

6 tablespoons plain yogurt
1 grapefruit
3½ ounce can tuna
1 bunch of watercress
2 avocados

1. Spoon the yogurt into a bowl. Cut all the skin and pith away from the grapefruit, and divide fruit into segments. Roughly chop flesh and add to yogurt.
2. Drain tuna and stir into yogurt, breaking up any large pieces.
3. Trim, wash and dry watercress. Reserve a few nice sprigs for garnish, then chop the rest and stir it into the yogurt. Cover and chill, unless serving immediately.
4. Halve avocados and remove stones. Spoon yogurt mixture on to each half and garnish with sprigs of watercress.

Not suitable for freezing.

Chicken, Melon and Kiwi Salad

A colourful and refreshing starter with a light minty dressing. Try to use a charentais melon, which has such a pretty orange–coloured flesh and a wonderfully fragrant flavour.

Serves 4–6
220–150 Calories a portion

UK

350g/12 oz cooked chicken (off the bone)
1 small melon
2–3 kiwi fruit
½ cucumber

DRESSING

150ml/¼ pint natural low-fat yogurt
1 tablespoon olive oil
1 tablespoon wine vinegar
1 teaspoon clear honey
small bunch of fresh mint or 1 teaspoon dried
freshly ground black pepper
sprigs of fresh mint, to garnish

US

12 ounces cooked chicken (off the bone)
1 small melon
2–3 kiwi fruit
½ cucumber

DRESSING

⅔ cup plain low-fat yogurt
1 tablespoon olive oil
1 tablespoon wine vinegar
1 teaspoon clear honey
small bunch of fresh mint or 1 teaspoon dried
freshly ground black pepper
sprigs of fresh mint, to garnish

1. Remove any skin from the chicken, then cut into neat bite-sized pieces.
2. Halve melon, remove seeds and scoop flesh into balls using a melon baller. Peel kiwi fruit and cut into large dice. Thinly slice cucumber.
3. Blend together the yogurt, oil, vinegar and honey for the dressing. Chop about 1 teaspoon of mint, if using fresh. Stir fresh or dried mint into dressing and season with pepper.
4. Combine chicken, melon and kiwi fruit, divide between serving dishes. Pour some dressing over each. Garnish each dish with slice of cucumber and sprigs of mint.

Not suitable for freezing.

MAIN MEALS

Beef and Lentil Chilli

This dish is similar to a Chilli con Carne, using chilli powder and cumin for seasoning, but with lentils rather than kidney beans. Using lentils also makes a good protein exchange for some of the meat, and makes the dish lower in fat and higher in fibre.

Serves 4
255 Calories a portion

UK	**US**
1 large onion	1 large onion
4 tomatoes	4 tomatoes
1 green pepper	1 green bell pepper
225g/8 oz lean minced beef	8 ounces lean ground beef
2 cloves garlic	2 cloves garlic
175g/6 oz split red lentils	¾ cup split red lentils
½ teaspoon ground cumin	½ teaspoon ground cumin
¼ teaspoon chilli powder	¼ teaspoon chilli powder
2 tablespoons tomato purée	2 tablespoons tomato paste
600ml/1 pint stock or water	2½ cups stock or water
small bunch of parsley	small bunch of parsley

1. Chop onion and tomatoes. Deseed and chop pepper.
2. Fry beef gently in a non-stick frying pan (skillet). Add the onions once the meat has started to brown. Crush in the garlic. There should be no need to add fat or oil because there is sufficient hidden fat in the meat. Cook gently until the onions soften.
3. Stir in the tomatoes and lentils. Add the spices and tomato purée (paste) to the stock and pour over the contents of the pan. Bring to the boil, then cover and simmer gently

for about 20 minutes, or until the lentils are mushy. Add the pepper for the last 10 minutes only, so that it retains its colour and bite.

4. Roughly chop a couple of tablespoons of parsley and stir in. Serve with wholewheat pasta or brown rice.

May be frozen. Use within 3 months.
Reheat from frozen in a covered dish in a moderate oven, until thoroughly heated through.
SHOPPING NOTE: Try a mixture of brown and wild rice, combining the unique character of wild rice with the nutty flavour and texture of long grain brown rice. You can buy it in ready-mixed boxes.

Spicy Mince With Potato Sticks————————

I love spicy food and using a good curry powder (or paste) is a quick and easy way of turning minced (ground) beef into something rather more interesting. Although curries are usually served with rice, my husband prefers potato, especially when they are cooked in this rather unusual way.

Serves 4
370 Calories a portion

UK

450g/1 lb lean minced beef
2 onions
2 cooking apples
1–2 tablespoons mild curry powder or
   paste
300ml/½ pint stock or water
2 tablespoons tomato purée
575 g/1¼ lb potatoes
½ teaspoon turmeric
½ teaspoon powdered ginger
a little cayenne or paprika pepper, to
   sprinkle

US

1 pound lean ground beef
2 onions
2 cooking apples
1–2 tablespoons mild curry powder or
   paste
1¼ cups stock or water
2 tablespoons tomato paste
1¼ pound potatoes
½ teaspoon turmeric
½ teaspoon powdered ginger
a little cayenne or paprika pepper, to
   sprinkle

1. Fry meat gently in a flameproof casserole (Dutch oven) until lightly browned. Meanwhile peel and chop the onions, then add to the casserole and continue to fry for a further few minutes.
2. Peel, core and chop the apples. Stir in the curry powder or paste, cook gently for 1 minute, then stir in the apples. Add the stock or water and tomato purée (paste), bring to the boil, then cover and cook gently for about 20 minutes.
3. Meanwhile peel the potatoes and cut them into sticks, like thick chips (French fries). Add turmeric and ginger to a pan of water, bring to the boil and add the potatoes. Cook for about 5 minutes until just tender. Drain.
4. Remove lid from casserole, scatter potatoes on top and serve sprinkled with a little cayenne or paprika pepper.

Freeze without potato topping. Use within 3 months.
Reheat from frozen in a covered casserole in a moderate oven, until thoroughly heated through.
Complete as above with spicy potato sticks.

Lamb and Bean Hot Pot

A warming and sustaining casserole of lean lamb, haricot (navy) beans and root vegetables which is delicious served with baked jacket potatoes and a green vegetable. Remember to soak the beans overnight first.

Serves 4
400 Calories a portion

UK	US
225g/8 oz dried haricot beans	1 cup dried navy beans
1 large onion	1 large onion
2 sticks celery	2 celery stalks
4 carrots	4 carrots
1 turnip (optional)	1 rutabaga/yellow turnip (optional)
2 cloves garlic	2 cloves garlic
4 lean lamb chops	4 lean lamb chops
600ml/1 pint light stock	2½ cups light stock
1 tablespoon tomato purée	1 tablespoon tomato paste
1 bouquet garni	1 bay leaf, sprig of thyme, sprigs of parsley
freshly ground black pepper	freshly ground black pepper
2 teaspoons cornflour	2 teaspoons cornstarch
small bunch parsley	small bunch parsley

1. Cover the beans with cold water and leave to soak overnight.
2. Slice the onion, chop the celery, peel and slice carrots and turnip, if using.
3. Trim off any fat on chops, then place in a heavy-based flameproof casserole (Dutch oven) and brown gently on both sides. There is no need to add any fat. Remove to a plate, leaving behind meat juices in the casserole.
4. Add onion, celery, carrots and turnip to the casserole and crush in the garlic. Sweat vegetables gently until softened and turning colour.
5. Return chops to the casserole and add stock, purée (paste) bouquet garni (herbs) and plenty of pepper. Drain and rinse beans and add these to the casserole, then bring to the boil. Turn down heat, cover and simmer for about 45 minutes or until the meat and beans are tender.

6. Blend cornflour (cornstarch) with a little water and stir into casserole to thicken. Chop parsley and sprinkle over before serving.

May be frozen. Use within 4 months.
Reheat from frozen, in a covered casserole, in a moderate oven until thoroughly heated through.

Spicy Lamb Koftas With Tomato and Yogurt Sauce

Koftas are small spicy meatballs threaded onto skewers and grilled (broiled). This recipe uses fresh coriander, but freshly–chopped mint or some minced fresh root ginger could be alternative flavourings. Serve with brown rice.

Serves 4
320 Calories a portion

UK	US
MEATBALLS:	**MEATBALLS:**
½ small onion	½ small onion
1 lemon	1 lemon
bunch of fresh coriander	bunch of fresh cilantro
450g/1 lb lean, minced lamb	1 pound lean ground beef
2 cloves garlic	2 cloves garlic
freshly ground black pepper	freshly ground black pepper
SAUCE:	SAUCE:
1 onion	1 onion
1 tablespoon sunflower oil	1 tablespoon sunflower oil
6 tasty tomatoes	6 flavourful tomatoes
1 tablespoon tomato purée	1 tablespoon tomato paste
freshly ground black pepper	freshly ground black pepper
pinch of sugar	pinch of sugar
150ml/¼ pint natural low-fat yogurt	⅔ cup plain low-fat yogurt

1. Chop the half onion very finely. Grate the lemon rind and finely chop about 2 tablespoons coriander (cilantro).
2. Place the lamb, onion, lemon rind and coriander (cilantro) in a bowl, crush in the garlic and season with pepper. Knead together with your hand (or briefly pound in a food processor).
3. Shape into small balls and thread onto skewers.

4. For the sauce, finely chop the onion, then cook in the oil for about 5 minutes until soft. Stir in the tomatoes, cook down, then add the tomato purée (paste) and season with pepper and sugar. Cook gently for about 15 minutes, then purée in a blender or food processor. Allow to cool, then stir in yogurt. Season with more pepper if necessary. Reheat gently.
5. Grill the meatballs for about 20 minutes until evenly browned, then serve with the warm sauce and brown rice.

Not suitable for freezing.

Pork Chow Mein

A dish made popular by Chinese take-away restaurants, but easy to prepare at home and a useful recipe for stretching a small amount of meat. Chicken could be substituted.

Serves 4   415 Calories a portion

UK

350g/12 oz lean boneless pork
1 small onion
1 green pepper
100g/4 oz button mushrooms
2 cloves garlic
1 tablespoon sunflower oil
1 tablespoon sesame oil
225g/8 oz wholewheat Chinese egg
    noodles
2–3 tablespoons sherry
2 tablespoons lemon juice

US

12 ounces lean boneless pork
1 small onion
1 green bell pepper
2 cups button mushrooms
2 cloves garlic
1 tablespoon sunflower oil
1 tablespoon sesame oil
8 ounces wholewheat Chinese egg
    noodles
2–3 tablespoons sherry
2 tablespoons lemon juice

1. Shred the pork into thin strips. Slice the onion, deseed and slice the pepper and slice the mushrooms. Crush garlic. Boil a large pan of water for the noodles.
2. Heat both the oils in a large wok or frying pan (skillet). Add the meat and stir-fry for about 5 minutes, until tender.
3. Drop noodles into pan of boiling water and cook for about 6 minutes until just tender.
4. Meanwhile, remove cooked pork to a warm plate and add the onion to the pan. Stir-fry for 1–2 minutes until slightly softened, then add the garlic, pepper and mushrooms. Stir-fry for a further 1–2 minutes.
5. Return pork to pan and add sherry and lemon juice. Toss everything together over a high heat.
6. Drain noodles. Toss with the pork and vegetables and serve immediately.

Not suitable for freezing.
COOK'S NOTE: Those who are not watching their salt intake may like to sprinkle this meal with a little soy sauce.

Chicken With Pineapple and Almonds

Although stir-frying is normally associated with Chinese dishes, this method can be used for cooking virtually any ingredients. Serve with brown rice.

Serves 4   405 Calories a portion

UK

3 large boned chicken breasts
small bunch fresh mint or 1 teaspoon
   dried
1 large red pepper
227g/8 oz can pineapple chunks, in fruit
   juice
25g/1 oz polyunsaturated margarine
50g/2 oz blanched almonds
2 tablespoons sunflower oil
2 tablespoons orange marmalade
sprigs of fresh mint, to garnish (optional)

US

3 large, boned chicken breasts
small bunch fresh mint or 1 teaspoon
   dried
1 large red bell pepper
8 ounce can pineapple chunks, in fruit
   juice
2½ tablespoons polyunsaturated
   margarine
½ cup blanched almonds
2 tablespoons sunflower oil
2 tablespoons orange marmalade
sprigs of fresh mint, to garnish (optional)

1. Skin the chicken breasts by holding the skin with a piece of kitchen towel (paper) and pulling gently. Cut chicken across into thin slices.
2. Chop the mint if using fresh — you need about 1 tablespoon. Slice pepper into strips and remove the seeds. Drain pineapple, reserving juice.
3. Melt margarine in a wok or frying pan (skillet), stir-fry the almonds quickly until golden. Remove to a plate.
4. Add oil to the wok, then add the chicken and mint and stir–fry for about 5 minutes until the chicken turns white and is cooked through.
5. Add pepper and pineapple chunks to the wok and toss everything together.
6. Blend marmalade with reserved pineapple juice, pour into pan and stir and toss over a high heat until the marmalade is dissolved. Return almonds to pan and serve immediately, garnished with sprigs of fresh mint, if liked.

Not suitable for freezing.

Stuffed Marrow (Summer Squash) With Tomato and Coriander Sauce

I developed this recipe at Harvest time when our farming friends were frequently leaving home-grown marrows (summer squash) on our doorstep.

Serves 4   200 Calories a portion

UK	US
1 medium onion	1 medium onion
1–2 cloves garlic	1–2 cloves garlic
1 leek	1 leek
450g/1 lb lean turkey mince	1 pound lean ground turkey
4 large, tasty tomatoes	4 large, tasty tomatoes
1 tablespoon tomato purée	1 tablespoon tomato paste
150ml/¼ pint vegetable stock	⅔ cup vegetable stock
bunch of fresh coriander	bunch of fresh cilantro
freshly ground black pepper	freshly ground black pepper
1 medium marrow	1 medium summer squash

1. Peel and chop onion. Peel and crush garlic. Slice and wash leek.
2. Dry–fry turkey in a non-stick pan (skillet). Add the onion, garlic and leek and continue to fry until the vegetables are soft.
3. Chop the tomatoes and stir in to the mixture with the tomato purée (paste) and stock. Chop about 3 tablespoons of coriander (cilantro) and add to the pan. Season to taste with pepper. Cook gently for 5 minutes.
4. Peel strips off marrow (squash) to produce a striped effect, then cut across into rings, about 5 cm (2 inches) wide. Scoop out seeds.
5. Lay marrow (squash) rings in a large, shallow ovenproof dish. Spoon turkey mixture into the centre of the rings and any remaining over the top. Cover with foil and bake at 180°C/350°F/Gas Mark 4 for 20 minutes. Serve with brown rice.

COOK'S NOTE: If fresh coriander (cilantro) is unavailable, substitute another fresh herb, such as basil or thyme.   Not suitable for freezing.

Mustard Crust Chicken

An incredibly quick recipe for jazzing up chicken portions. It's one which we've frequently enjoyed on summer holidays, when nobody wants to spend a lot of time in the kitchen. Serve with a salad and some good, freshly-baked wholemeal (wholewheat) bread.

Serves 4   195 Calories a portion

UK

3 tablespoons French mustard
15g/½ oz polyunsaturated margarine
1 lemon
freshly ground black pepper
4 skinned chicken portions

US

3 tablespoons French mustard
1 generous tablespoon polyunsaturated
  margarine
1 lemon
freshly ground black pepper
4 skinned chicken portions

1. Mix together the mustard and margarine. Grate lemon rind and squeeze juice and add to the mustard. Season mixture with pepper.
2. Spread the mustard mixture over the chicken portions and leave to marinate for a couple of hours, if time allows.
3. Place chicken on a rack over a grill (broiling) pan and cook under a moderate grill for about 20 minutes, turning from time to time, until cooked right through.

Not suitable for freezing.

Ginger and Orange Chicken With Dried Fruits

Prunes, apricots and spices cooked with plain ordinary chicken portions make a delicious, subtly flavoured Middle Eastern dish. Serve with a mixture of brown and wild rice.

Serves 2

305 Calories a portion

UK

2 chicken portions
50g/2 oz no-need-to-soak dried apricots
50g/2 oz no-need-to-soak dried prunes
small piece fresh ginger
1 orange
300ml/½ pint chicken stock or water
1 tablespoon cider vinegar
1 tablespoon apricot jam
freshly ground black pepper
2 teaspoons cornflour

US

2 chicken portions
½ cup no-need-to-soak dried apricots
½ cup no-need-to-soak dried prunes
small piece fresh ginger
1 orange
1¼ cups chicken stock or water
1 tablespoon cider vinegar
1 tablespoon apricot jam
freshly ground black pepper
2 teaspoons cornstarch

1. Skin the chicken portions and place in an ovenproof casserole with the apricots and prunes.
2. Peel and finely chop the ginger. Grate the rind and squeeze the juice from the orange.
3. Blend together in a jug the stock, vinegar, jam, ginger, orange juice and rind and pour into the casserole. Season with plenty of pepper, then cover.
4. Cook at 190°C/375°F/Gas Mark 5 for 45 minutes to 1 hour, until the chicken is thoroughly cooked through.
5. Blend the cornflour (cornstarch) with a little water. Stir some of the casserole liquid into the slaked cornflour, then pour into the casserole, stirring until thickened.

May be frozen. Use within 3 months.
Defrost completely in the refrigerator, then reheat in a moderate oven until thoroughly heated through.

Turkey and Three Vegetable Stir-Fry_____

A super-fast dish using lean turkey (or chicken if preferred) with a colourful selection of vegetables. These can be varied but, for maximum appeal, keep to contrasting colours.

Serves 2
390 Calories a portion

UK	US
225g/8 oz turkey breast fillet	8 ounces turkey breast fillet (uncooked)
1 tablespoon cornflour	1 tablespoon cornstarch
1 large clove garlic	1 large clove garlic
small piece fresh root ginger	small piece fresh root ginger
100g/4 oz broccoli florets	1 cup broccoli florets
6 fresh baby corn	6 fresh baby corn
50g/2 oz mushrooms	1 cup mushrooms
1 tablespoon sunflower oil	1 tablespoon sunflower oil
1 tablespoon sesame oil	1 tablespoon sesame oil
100ml/4 fl oz dry white wine	½ cup dry white wine
1 teaspoon clear honey	1 teaspoon clear honey

1. Slice the turkey crossways into thin strips, then toss in the cornflour (cornstarch).
2. Crush the garlic and peel and finely mince the ginger. Slice the broccoli lengthways and each baby corn diagonally into four. Slice the mushrooms.
3. Heat the oils in a wok or large frying pan (skillet). Add the turkey, garlic and ginger, and stir-fry for 3–4 minutes until the turkey is tender. Push to one side or remove to a plate.
4. Add the broccoli and corn to the wok, stir-fry for 1 minute, then add the wine and honey and cook over a high heat stirring until the vegetables are just tender but still retaining some bite. The wine should have reduced down to just a couple of tablespoons.
5. Stir in the mushrooms, return the turkey and stir-fry together for a further minute, then serve immediately.

Not suitable for freezing.

Chicken and Mango Risotto

A useful recipe for stretching chicken portions to serve four people. The mangoes add a welcome juiciness to the rice — peaches or apricots could be substituted. You can use all brown rice or a more exotic blend of brown and wild rice.

Serves 4
540 Calories a portion

UK	**US**
2 skinned chicken breasts (about 350g/12 oz)	2 skinned chicken breasts (about 12 ounces)
1 large leek	1 large leek
25g/1 oz polyunsaturated margarine	2½ tablespoons polyunsaturated margarine
1 tablespoon sunflower oil	1 tablespoon sunflower oil
40g/1½ oz flaked almonds	⅓ cup slivered almonds
225g/8 oz brown and wild rice	1 cup brown and wild rice
50g/2 oz raisins	⅓ cup raisins
420g/15 oz can mangoes	15 ounce can mangoes
600ml/1 pint chicken stock (or half dry white wine and stock)	2½ cups chicken stock (or half dry white wine and stock)

1. Slice the chicken crossways into strips. Slice leek and wash thoroughly in a sieve (wire mesh colander) under running water.
2. Heat margarine and oil in a deep frying pan (skillet), add the almonds and sauté briefly until golden. Drain on kitchen paper.
3. Add chicken and leek to pan and fry gently for about 5 minutes. Stir in the rice and raisins and fry for a further minute.
4. Drain the mango juice into a jug and add the stock (or wine and stock). Pour into pan, bring to the boil, then turn down heat, cover and cook gently for 35 minutes. Top up with more stock if necessary but, by the time the rice is tender, all the liquid should be absorbed.
5. Chop mangoes into bite-sized pieces, stir into rice mixture and heat through. Serve scattered with toasted almonds.

May be frozen. Use within 2 months.
Thaw overnight in the refrigerator. Reheat in a covered dish in a moderate oven until thoroughly heated through. Complete with fresh toasted almonds.

Stir–Fried Chicken Livers

A super-quick dish. Serve with brown rice and a refreshing green salad.

Serves 4
180 Calories a portion

UK	US
350g/12 oz chicken livers	12 ounces chicken livers
1 red pepper	1 red bell pepper
2 leeks	2 leeks
2 courgettes	2 zucchini
1 tablespoon walnut or sunflower oil	1 tablespoon walnut or sunflower oil
large pinch of dried sage	large pinch of dried sage
1 clove garlic	1 clove garlic
2 tablespoons dry sherry	2 tablespoons dry sherry

1. Trim the livers and slice thinly.
2. Deseed pepper and slice into thin strips. Trim ends of leeks and courgettes (zucchini) and slice diagonally.
3. Heat the oil in a non-stick frying pan (skillet). Add the livers and the sage, crush in the garlic and lightly sauté for about 3 minutes only, until browned on the outside but still pink and tender within. Remove to a plate.
4. Add the vegetables to the pan and cook for about 5 minutes, stirring occasionally, until just softened. Return livers to pan, add sherry and heat through. Serve immediately.

Not suitable for freezing.

Tandoori Chicken

You can buy ready-made Tandoori mixes, but like so many commercial products, they contain a fair amount of salt. The mix is very easy to prepare and the flavour from the spices certainly discounts the need for any salt. This marinade works equally well with pork and fish. Serve with a green salad, rice and perhaps some warm naan bread (available from larger supermarkets and ethnic stores).

Serves 4
165 Calories a portion

UK

4 chicken portions
1 lemon

MARINADE:

8 cardamom pods
small piece fresh root ginger
1½ teaspoons paprika
1 teaspoon ground cumin
1 teaspoon ground coriander
¼ teaspoon ground cinnamon
½ teaspoon ground allspice
¼ teaspoon chilli powder
freshly ground black pepper
150ml/¼ pint natural low-fat yogurt
4 cloves garlic

GARNISH:

1 small onion
1 lemon
flat leaf parsley or fresh coriander

US

4 chicken portions
1 lemon

MARINADE:

8 cardamom pods
small piece fresh root ginger
1½ teaspoons paprika
1 teaspoon ground cumin
1 teaspoon ground coriander
¼ teaspoon ground cinnamon
½ teaspoon ground allspice
¼ teaspoon chilli powder
freshly ground black pepper
⅔ cup plain low-fat yogurt
4 cloves garlic

GARNISH:

1 small onion
1 lemon
flat leaf parsley or fresh cilantro

1. Skin the chicken, then slash each portion several times with a sharp knife. Squeeze lemon juice, pour over chicken, cover and leave in the refrigerator while preparing the marinade.
2. Crush cardamoms, discard the shells and crush the seeds. Peel and finely chop ginger. Combine cardamom and ginger with remaining spices, grinding in some pepper.
3. Stir spices into yogurt and crush in the garlic.
4. Pour yogurt mixture over chicken, turning it over several times to make sure it's thoroughly coated. Cover and leave to marinate, preferably overnight, or for several hours in the refrigerator.
5. Place chicken on a grill (broiling) rack, leaving behind the excess marinade and cook under a moderate grill for 20–25 minutes, turning after 10 minutes, until thoroughly cooked through. Alternatively, it can be baked on a rack over a baking tin (pan) at 200°C/400°F/Gas Mark 6 for 30–40 minutes.
6. Slice onion and cut lemon into wedges and use to garnish with sprigs of parsley or coriander (cilantro).

Not suitable for freezing.

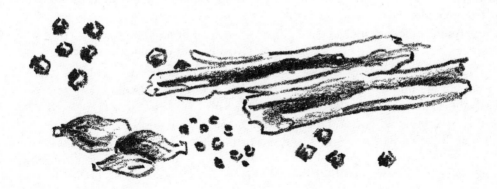

Baked Stuffed Trout

Trout is most often served grilled (broiled) and topped with sautéed almonds. Here's a delicious way of serving it which is more unusual and ideal for dinner parties. Don't be put off by gutting and boning, a fishmonger (dealer) will always prepare the fish for you.

Serves 4
245 Calories a portion

UK

4 fresh trout, about 225g/8 oz each

STUFFING:

1 large leek
2 tomatoes
1 clove garlic
25g/1 oz polyunsaturated margarine
small piece of fresh root ginger
1 lemon
small bunch of fresh mint or 1 teaspoon
    dried
25g/1 oz porridge oats
freshly ground black pepper

US

4 fresh trout, about 8 ounces each

STUFFING:

1 large leek
2 tomatoes
1 clove garlic
2½ tablespoons polyunsaturated
    margarine
small piece of fresh root ginger
1 lemon
small bunch of fresh mint or 1 teaspoon
    dried
⅓ cup rolled oats
freshly ground black pepper

1. Clean and gut trout by slitting the fish along the belly with a sharp knife, then scraping out and discarding the entrails. Rinse under cold running water. You can ask the fishmonger (dealer) to do this for you. You can now stuff the fish or, if preferred, bone it first. To bone, first cut off head, tail and fins. Then, open out the fish and spread flat, skin side up. Press firmly down the backbone to loosen it, then turn the fish over and gradually ease away the bone, using a sharp knife. Remove as many small bones as possible, then fold back into original shape. The fishmonger will also do this for you.

2. For the stuffing, slice the leek. Peel and chop tomatoes. Crush garlic. Melt margarine

in a small pan, add the leek and cook until softened. Then add the tomatoes and garlic and cook gently for a few minutes more, to soften the tomatoes.

3. Peel and finely chop ginger, grate rind from lemon and squeeze juice. Chop about 1 tablespoon fresh mint.
4. Take pan off heat and stir in the remaining stuffing ingredients and season with pepper.
5. Divide stuffing between the fish, neatly shaping them again afterwards.
6. Place fish in a lightly-greased ovenproof dish, cover with foil and bake at 190°C/375°F/Gas Mark 5 for 30–40 minutes, until the fish is cooked.

Not suitable for freezing.

Sweet and Sour Fish

A very simple dish for transforming some fairly ordinary fish, such as cod or haddock, into a tasty meal. Serve with brown rice.

Serves 4   255 Calories a portion

UK

1 onion
1 red or green pepper
350g/12 oz button mushrooms
25g/1 oz polyunsaturated margarine
1 tablespoon sunflower oil
1 tablespoon clear honey
2 tablespoons cider vinegar
2 tablespoons tomato purée
675g/1½ lb cod fillet
freshly ground black pepper

US

1 onion
1 red or green bell pepper
12 ounces button mushrooms
2½ tablespoons polyunsaturated
  margarine
1 tablespoon sunflower oil
1 tablespoon clear honey
2 tablespoons cider vinegar
2 tablespoons tomato paste
1½ pounds cod fillet
freshly ground black pepper

1. Slice onions, pepper and mushrooms. Heat margarine and oil in a small pan and cook the onion until softened. Add the pepper and mushrooms and cook for a further few minutes.
2. Blend together the honey, vinegar and tomato purée (paste), add to pan and warm through.
3. Place the fish in a shallow ovenproof dish and season well with freshly ground black pepper. Pour over sweet and sour vegetable mixture.
3. Cover and bake for about 30 minutes at 170°C/325°F/Gas Mark 3, until the fish is tender.

Not suitable for freezing.

Fish and Mushroom Pie

White fish (such as cod or haddock) in a slightly piquant mushroom sauce topped with sliced par-boiled potatoes then finished off in the oven. Serve with some lightly cooked spring greens or other fresh, seasonal green vegetable.

Serves 4   455 Calories a portion

UK

675g/1½ lb white fish
675g/1½ lb potatoes
40g/1½ oz polyunsaturated margarine
100g/4 oz button mushrooms
1 red pepper
40g/1½ oz wholemeal flour
450ml/¾ pint semi-skimmed milk
1 tablespoon tomato purée
2 teaspoons Worcestershire sauce
freshly ground black pepper

US

1½ pounds white fish
1½ pounds potatoes
4 scant tablespoons polyunsaturated
   margarine
2 cups button mushrooms
1 red bell pepper
⅓ cup wholewheat flour
2 cups low-fat milk
1 tablespoon tomato paste
2 teaspoons Worcestershire sauce
freshly ground black pepper

1. Skin fish and remove any bones. Cut into large bite-sized pieces and place in an ovenproof dish.
2. Scrub potatoes (there's no need to peel them) then slice. Par-boil in a pan of boiling water for about 5 minutes until just tender then drain.
3. Slice mushrooms and dice pepper.
4. Melt margarine in a small pan, stir in the mushrooms and cook gently for 3–4 minutes. Take pan off heat and stir in flour. Return to heat and cook for 1 minute. Remove pan from heat and gradually blend in milk. Heat, stirring continuously until thickened. Stir in diced pepper, tomato purée (paste) and Worcestershire sauce.
5. Pour sauce over fish and arrange potatoes, overlapping on top. Grind over some pepper. Bake at 190°C/375°F/Gas Mark 5 for 30 minutes until fish is tender.

Not suitable for freezing.

Plaice With Mustard and Orange Sauce____

A good tangy sauce for those who prefer their food dressed up rather than served plain.
Accompany with a good helping of fresh vegetables.

Serves 4   335 Calories a portion

UK

300ml/½ pint dry cider
2 oranges
1 bay leaf
675g/1½ lb plaice fillets
freshly ground black pepper
40g/1½ oz polyunsaturated margarine
25g/1 oz wholewheat flour
1 teaspoon wholegrain mustard
2 teaspoons brown sugar
freshly chopped parsley, to garnish

US

1¼ cups dry cider
2 oranges
1 bay leaf
1½ pounds plaice fillets
freshly ground black pepper
3½ tablespoons polyunsaturated
  margarine
¼ cup wholewheat flour
1 teaspoon wholegrain mustard
2 teaspoons brown sugar
freshly chopped parsley, to garnish

1. Pour the cider into a deep frying pan (skillet). Grate the rind from one of the oranges and squeeze the juice of both. Add rind and juice to the pan. Add bay leaf and bring to the boil.
2. Turn down heat, add fish and season well with pepper. Cook gently for 10–15 minutes, until the fish is tender.
3. Meanwhile, melt the margarine in a pan. Remove from heat, stir in the flour and cook over a low heat for 1 minute.
4. Remove fish from cooking liquor, cover fish and keep warm. Discard bay leaf. Stir the liquor into the roux mixture, return to the heat and cook, stirring continuously, until thickened.
5. Stir mustard and sugar into sauce and check seasoning, adding more pepper if necessary. Pour sauce over fish and serve immediately lightly dusted with parsley.

Not suitable for freezing.

Cheesy Crumb-Topped Fish Casserole_____

One of the beauties of fish is that it is so quick to cook. This dish requires very little preparation. Use any white fish, such as cod or haddock, and simply cook it in a casserole with cider and vegetables, then top with cheesy breadcrumbs. Finish under the grill.

Serves 4   290 Calories a portion

UK	US
675g/1½ lb white fish fillet	1½ pounds white fish fillet
1 onion	1 onion
100g/4 oz mushrooms	4 ounces mushrooms
4 tomatoes	4 tomatoes
2 tablespoons sunflower oil	2 tablespoons sunflower oil
150ml/¼ pint dry cider	⅔ cup dry cider
½ teaspoon dried oregano	½ teaspoon dried oregano
freshly ground black pepper	freshly ground black pepper
50g/2 oz fresh wholewheat breadcrumbs	1 cup fresh wholewheat breadcrumbs
25g/1 oz grated Cheddar cheese	¼ cup grated Cheddar cheese
2 teaspoons freshly grated Parmesan cheese	2 teaspoons freshly grated Parmesan cheese

1. Skin the fish and remove any bones. Cut up into pieces and place in an ovenproof casserole.
2. Slice the onion, mushrooms and tomatoes.
3. Heat the oil in a small pan and lightly cook the onion until softened. Stir in the mushrooms and cook for 1 minute more. Pour in the cider, add oregano and season with pepper. Bring to the boil. Turn off heat.
4. Lay tomatoes on top of fish and pour over hot cider and vegetables. Cover and cook at 180°C/350°F/Gas Mark 4 for about 25 minutes, or until the fish is tender.
5. Meanwhile combine Cheddar cheese with the breadcrumbs and Parmesan cheese. Sprinkle over the fish and pop under the grill to brown. Serve immediately.

Not suitable for freezing.

Bean and Lentil Dal

A spicy vegetarian curry which, served with some rice or a baked jacket potato and a yogurt side dish (see Minty Potato Raita), makes a very sustaining meal. Split lentils are quick to cook, but note that you will need to soak the beans overnight before using them.

Serves 4
335 Calories a portion

UK	US
175g/6 oz dried red kidney beans	1 cup dried red kidney beans
1 large onion	1 large onion
2 cloves garlic	2 cloves garlic
small piece fresh ginger	small piece fresh ginger
1 chilli	1 chilli
2 tablespoons sunflower oil	2 tablespoons sunflower oil
1 tablespoon curry paste (mild, medium or hot, as preferred)	1 tablespoon curry paste (mild, medium or hot, as preferred)
1 teaspoon turmeric	1 teaspoon turmeric
1 teaspoon ground cumin	1 teaspoon ground cumin
175g/6 oz red split lentils	¾ cup red split lentils
700ml/1¼ pints vegetable stock or water	3 cups vegetable stock or water
1 tablespoon tomato purée	1 tablespoon tomato paste
½ green pepper	½ green bell pepper
2–3 tomatoes	2–3 tomatoes

1. Soak beans overnight in cold water.
2. Next day, drain beans, then place in a pan with fresh water, bring to the boil and boil rapidly for 10 minutes. Turn down heat and continue cooking for a further hour.
3. Meanwhile, start making the dal. Slice the onion, crush the garlic, peel and finely mince the ginger and finely chop the chilli, discarding the seeds. (Do not touch your eyes while preparing the chilli — it will sting.) Wash hands and continue.
4. Heat the oil in a large saucepan and fry the onion, garlic, ginger and chilli for a few minutes until the onion is softened. Stir in the curry paste, cook for a further minute, then stir in the turmeric and cumin.

5. Add the lentils, stir around to coat in the spice mixture, then pour in the stock or water and add the tomato purée (paste). Bring to the boil, cover and simmer for 15 minutes.
6. Meanwhile, chop and deseed the pepper and roughly chop the tomatoes. Drain kidney beans.
7. Add pepper, tomatoes and beans to the dal mixture and cook for a further 5–10 minutes until the lentils are mushy.

May be frozen. Use within 3 months.
Reheat from frozen in a covered dish in a moderate oven until thoroughly heated through.

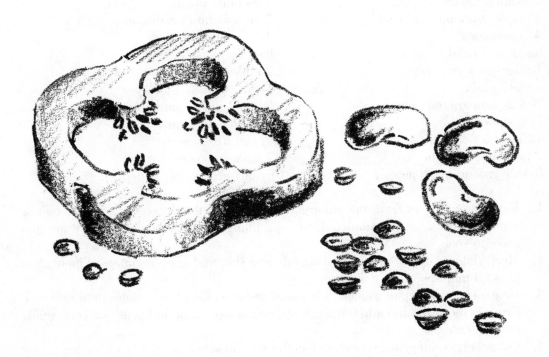

Baked Stuffed Aubergines

This recipe is based on the Turkish dish Imam Bayeldi but doesn't use the high quantity of oil. It makes a good vegetarian main course dish served with some brown rice tossed with a selection of nuts and a dollop of low-fat natural (plain) yogurt.

Serves 4
100 Calories a portion

UK

2 aubergines
1 medium onion
175g/6 oz button mushrooms
4–5 tomatoes
handful of parsley
1 tablespoon olive oil
1 clove garlic
¼ teaspoon ground cinnamon
½ teaspoon sugar
125g/4 oz frozen peas
2 tablespoons raisins
freshly ground black pepper

US

2 eggplants
1 medium onion
3 cups button mushrooms
4–5 tomatoes
handful of parsley
1 tablespoon olive oil
1 clove garlic
¼ teaspoon ground cinnamon
½ teaspoon sugar
⅔ cup frozen peas
2 tablespoons raisins
freshly ground black pepper

1. Remove leaf bases from the aubergines (eggplants) then place in a pan of boiling water and cook for 10 minutes. Drain and plunge immediately into cold water and leave to cool.
2. Meanwhile, chop onion and mushrooms and skin and chop tomatoes. Finely chop about 3 tablespoons of parsley.
3. Heat oil in a frying pan (skillet), add onion and cook for a few minutes until softened. Crush in the garlic and add the tomatoes, cinnamon, sugar and peas and cook gently for 5 minutes.
4. Cut aubergines (eggplants) in half lengthways and scoop out the flesh leaving a 1cm (½ inch) thick shell. Arrange shells in a lightly oiled ovenproof dish and season inside with pepper.

5. Chop aubergine flesh and stir into the onion and tomato mixture together with the mushrooms, raisins and parsley. Season generously with pepper. Stir round and cook gently for a couple of minutes.

6. Pile mixture into the aubergine (eggplant) shells, cover and bake for about 20 minutes at 190°C/375°F/Gas Mark 5.

Not suitable for freezing.

Vegetable and Pasta Casserole

This vegetarian recipe can be varied to use any pulses, pasta or vegetables you have available. The dried beans will need soaking overnight. If you forget, see Cook's Note below.

Serves 4–6
290–195 Calories a portion

UK

100g/4 oz dried haricot or butter beans
1 large onion
4 tomatoes
2 sticks celery
½ fennel bulb (optional)
2 tablespoons olive oil
1 clove garlic
1.1 litres/2 pints vegetable stock
2 tablespoons tomato purée
1 teaspoon dried basil
freshly ground black pepper
225g/8 oz carrots
100g/4 oz wholewheat macaroni
100g/4 oz frozen peas
freshly grated Parmesan cheese, to serve
   (optional)

US

½ cup dried navy or lima beans
1 large onion
4 tomatoes
2 stalks celery
½ fennel bulb (optional)
2 tablespoons olive oil
1 clove garlic
5 cups vegetable stock
2 tablespoons tomato paste
1 teaspoon dried basil
freshly ground black pepper
8 ounces carrots
1 cup wholewheat macaroni
1 cup frozen peas
freshly grated Parmesan cheese, to serve
   (optional)

1. Soak the beans overnight in cold water.
2. Chop the onion, skin and chop tomatoes and trim and slice celery and fennel, if using. Heat the oil in a large saucepan or flameproof casserole (Dutch oven), add the onion, celery and fennel and crush in the garlic. Sweat for about 5 minutes.
3. Stir in the tomatoes, stock, tomato purée (paste), drained beans, basil and plenty of pepper. Bring to the boil, then turn down heat, cover and simmer for 1 hour until the beans are tender.

4. Peel and slice the carrots. Then when the beans are cooked, add the carrots and macaroni to the pan. Cover and simmer for 10 minutes, then add the peas, bring back to the boil and simmer for a further 5 minutes, until all the ingredients are tender. Season to taste with more pepper, if required.
5. Serve sprinkled with a little Parmesan cheese and warm wholemeal bread.

May be frozen. Use within 2 months.
Reheat gently from frozen in a covered dish in a moderate oven until thoroughly heated through.

COOK'S NOTE: If you should forget to soak the beans, cover them with cold water in a pan, bring to the boil and simmer for 5 minutes. Then remove pan from heat and leave them to soak for 2 hours. Then continue as above.

Khichhari

This is a spicy Middle Eastern dish of rice and lentils. For me it always conjures up memories of a holiday in Cairo where the sky was brilliantly blue and there was a fascinating cosmopolitan mass of people. There, sitting outside the Nile Hilton, one could choose Falafel (chick-pea rissoles in Arab bread), charcoal-cooked lamb kebabs or Khichhari from one of the street-food vendors. It was a difficult decision, all were delicious — and embarrassingly cheap. I hope one day I'll have the pleasure of re-living that wonderful experience.

Serves 4
340 Calories a portion

UK	US
1 large onion	1 large onion
2 tablespoons sunflower oil	2 tablespoons sunflower oil
4–5 cardamom pods	4–5 cardamom pods
½ teaspoon coriander seeds	½ teaspoon coriander seeds
½ teaspoon cumin seeds	½ teaspoon cumin seeds
small piece fresh root ginger	small piece fresh root ginger
½ cinnamon stick	½ cinnamon stick
1 clove garlic	1 clove garlic
100g/4 oz brown rice	½ cup brown rice
850ml/1½ pints vegetable stock	3¾ cups vegetable stock
½ teaspoon turmeric	½ teaspoon turmeric
100g/4 oz split lentils	½ cup split lentils
25g/1 oz flaked almonds	¼ cup slivered almonds
50g/2 oz raisins	⅓ cup raisins

1. Slice the onion. Heat the oil in a large saucepan, add the onions and cook gently until softened.
2. Remove cardamom pods and crush the seeds with the coriander and cumin, using a pestle and mortar or a coffee grinder. Peel and finely chop ginger.
3. Add all the spices, except the turmeric, to the onion, crush in the garlic and stir around for 1–2 minutes.

4. Stir in the rice, mix well then pour in stock and add the turmeric. Bring to the boil, then cover with a tight-fitting lid and simmer for 15 minutes.
5. Add lentils to pan and cook for a further 20 minutes, until the rice and lentils are tender and all the stock is absorbed. (Add a little more stock if necessary.)
6. Toast almonds under the grill (broiler) until golden. Tip rice mixture into a serving dish and scatter almonds and raisins over the top. If liked, serve with some natural (plain) yogurt.

May be frozen. Use within 2 months.
Thaw overnight in the refrigerator. Reheat gently in a covered dish in a moderate oven. Complete with freshly-toasted almonds and raisins.

Vegetarian Pizza

Home-made pizza is very quick to produce using a packet of bread mix. Try this delicious topping of tomato, mushrooms, pepper, pineapple and mozzarella cheese for that wonderful stringy effect. Serve with a side salad.

Serves 4–6
435–290 Calories a portion

UK

BASE:

280g/10 oz packet wholemeal bread mix
1 tablespoon sunflower oil

TOPPING:

1 medium onion
1 tablespoon olive oil
1 clove garlic
400g/14 oz can tomatoes
1 tablespoon freshly chopped basil or ½
   teaspoon dried
freshly ground black pepper
1 small green pepper
100g/4 oz button mushrooms
226g/8 oz can pineapple pieces in
   natural juice
75g/3 oz mozzarella cheese

US

BASE:

10 ounce packet wholewheat bread mix
1 tablespoon sunflower oil

TOPPING:

1 medium onion
1 tablespoon olive oil
1 clove garlic
14 ounce can tomatoes
1 tablespoon freshly chopped basil or ½
   teaspoon dried
freshly ground black pepper
1 small green bell pepper
2 cups button mushrooms
8 ounce can pineapple pieces in natural
   juice
3 ounces mozzarella cheese

1. First prepare the topping. Chop the onion and cook in the oil until softened. Crush in the garlic, drain tomatoes, chop and add to the pan and season with basil and pepper. Cook for about 5 minutes until thick and pulpy.
2. Deseed and finely chop green (bell) pepper. Slice mushrooms.
3. Make up bread mix as directed on the packet. Knead for 5 minutes by hand until smooth and elastic. (This can be done using a dough hook in an electric mixer.) Roll

out to a 25cm (10 inch) round and place on an oiled baking sheet. Brush with oil to seal.

4. Cover with tomato and onion mixture, leaving a 1cm (½ inch) rim round the outside. Scatter peppers and mushrooms over the top. Drain pineapple and scatter over the pizza. Grind over some black pepper.

5. Slice cheese thinly and arrange evenly over the top then cover with an oiled polythene bag and leave to rise in a warm place for 20–30 minutes, until doubled in size.

6. Uncover and bake at 220°C/425°F/Gas Mark 7 for 25–30 minutes.

May be frozen. Cool and open-freeze then wrap. Use within 3 months. Reheat from frozen in a moderately hot oven for about 35 minutes.

Macaroni and Vegetable Layer

A substantial vegetarian dish of macaroni in a leek sauce on a bed of various vegetables, then topped with a cheesy crumb and grilled until crisp.

Serves 4–6
435–290 Calories a portion

UK	US
175g/6 oz wholewheat macaroni	1½ cups wholewheat macaroni
100g/4 oz broccoli	4 ounces broccoli
2 courgettes	2 zucchini
2 leeks	2 leeks
freshly ground black pepper	freshly ground black pepper
50g/2 oz polyunsaturated margarine	¼ cup polyunsaturated margarine
50g/2 oz wholemeal flour	½ cup wholewheat flour
450ml/¾ pint semi-skimmed milk	2 cups low-fat milk
½ teaspoon dried oregano	½ teaspoon dried oregano
400g/14 oz can tomatoes	14 ounce can tomatoes
50g/2 oz fresh wholemeal breadcrumbs	1 cup fresh wholewheat breadcrumbs
2 tablespoons grated Parmesan cheese	2 tablespoons grated Parmesan cheese

1. Cook macaroni in boiling water for about 10 minutes until just tender.
2. Meanwhile roughly chop broccoli and slice courgettes (zucchini) and leeks. Lightly cook broccoli and courgettes in a little boiling water or steam or microwave. Wash leeks thoroughly.
3. Drain pasta. Drain vegetables and place in a large heatproof serving dish. Season with pepper. Cover to keep warm.
4. Melt margarine in a small pan, add the leeks and cook until soft. Off the heat, stir in the flour then cook for 1 minute, stirring. Remove pan from heat again and gradually blend in the milk. Return to heat and cook, stirring continuously until thickened. Season with oregano and plenty of pepper. Leave on a low heat to keep warm.
5. Tip tomatoes into a pan and heat. Using a draining spoon, spoon tomatoes into dish with vegetables. Stir excess juice into leek sauce.

6. Stir macaroni into leek sauce and pour over vegetables. Mix together breadcrumbs and Parmesan and sprinkle over. Place under the grill until golden or bake in a moderately hot oven if you want to keep the dish hot for a while before serving.

May be frozen (best without crumb topping). Use within 2–3 months.
Reheat thoroughly for about 1 hour in a moderate oven with a fresh crumb and cheese topping.

Potato and Pesto Egg Nests

One of my favourite dishes as a child was a nest of mashed potato with a poached egg in the middle. Here, for more adult tastes, I've added a little pesto sauce to the potato, which is then turned into individual serving dishes and the egg is baked in it. Serve with a home-made tomato sauce and perhaps a green side salad.

Serves 2
270 Calories a portion

UK

450g/1 lb potatoes
3 tablespoons natural low-fat yogurt
1 tablespoon pesto sauce
2 fresh eggs
freshly ground black pepper

US

1 pound potatoes
3 tablespoons plain low-fat yogurt
1 tablespoon pesto sauce
2 fresh eggs
freshly ground black pepper

1. Peel potatoes and cut up, if large. Place in a pan of boiling water and cook until tender.
2. Drain potatoes then mash with yogurt and pesto sauce.
3. Divide potato mixture between two individual heatproof dishes, making a depression in the middle of the potato.
4. Drop an egg into each depression and grind over some pepper. Bake at 190°C/375°F/Gas Mark 5 for 15–20 minutes until the eggs are just set. Serve immediately.

Not suitable for freezing

COOK'S NOTE: Pesto sauce is made from a delicious mixture of basil, pine nuts and Parmesan cheese. You can buy it in jars in good supermarkets and delicatessens. It does contain added salt but as only a small amount is added to the potato, this is quite acceptable. Moreover, there's no need to salt the potatoes when they are cooking.

VEGETABLES AND ACCOMPANIMENTS

These are slightly special recipes for when you want to serve something a little different or for when you are entertaining. For most meals, however, vegetables should be lightly boiled, steamed or microwaved and served simply.

Pepperonata

If like me you can't resist the fabulous vibrant colours of multi-coloured peppers — green, red, yellow and orange — this classic Italian dish makes a popular accompaniment to grilled and baked food. Those not watching their salt intake can stir in some black olives for real authenticity. This is a convenient dish for entertaining as the quantity can be easily increased to serve as many as required. It can be prepared in advance and served hot or cold.

Serves 4
90 Calories a portion

UK

1 large onion
1–2 cloves garlic
3 peppers (1 red, 1 yellow or orange, 1 green)
2 tablespoons olive oil
350g/12 oz ripe tomatoes
½ teaspoon dried basil
freshly ground black pepper

US

1 large onion
1–2 cloves garlic
3 bell peppers (1 red, 1 yellow or orange, 1 green)
2 tablespoons olive oil
12 ounces ripe tomatoes
½ teaspoon dried basil
freshly ground black pepper

1. Peel and slice the onion. Peel and crush the garlic. Deseed and slice the peppers.
2. Heat the oil in a saucepan or flameproof casserole (Dutch oven), add the onion, garlic and peppers, cover and cook gently for about 15 minutes.
3. Place the tomatoes in a bowl, pour over boiling water, then drain and fill bowl with cold water. Slip off tomato skins, discard and roughly chop the flesh.
4. Add tomatoes and basil to the pan, season with pepper, then cover and leave to cook gently for a further 20 minutes.

May be frozen. Use within 2–3 months.
Thaw overnight in the refrigerator, then reheat gently, if to be served warm.

Sesame Stir-Fried Vegetables

Stir-frying is now recognized as one of the best ways of cooking. Not only is it quick, but it retains the colour, texture and nutrient value of the vegetables. You can use any colourful selection of fresh seasonal vegetables. Crisp, longer cooking vegetables should always be the first into the pan, followed by quicker cooking ones, so they all retain their 'bite'.

Serves 4
105 Calories a portion

UK	**US**
225g/8 oz broccoli	8 ounces broccoli
225g/8 oz carrots	8 ounces carrots
4 sticks celery	4 celery stalks
1 tablespoon sesame seeds	1 tablespoon sesame seeds
1 tablespoon sunflower oil	1 tablespoon sunflower oil
1 tablespoon sesame oil	1 tablespoon sesame oil
1 clove garlic	1 clove garlic
juice of 1 lemon	juice of 1 lemon

1. Cut the broccoli heads into small florets and slice the stems thinly. Cut the carrots and celery into thin julienne sticks (like matchsticks).
2. Scatter the sesame seeds on a baking sheet and brown them under the grill (broiler).
3. Heat the oil in a wok or large frying pan (skillet). Crush in the garlic, then add the broccoli stems and carrots. Add lemon juice and stir-fry for a few minutes. Then add the celery and finally the broccoli florets. If necessary, add a couple of tablespoons of water. Cover and steam vegetables for just a minute or two to tenderize them.
3. Serve immediately sprinkled with sesame seeds.

Not suitable for freezing.

Leek, Nut and Mushroom Stir-Fry

This is a quick way of providing a dish of cooked vegetables and a favourite family recipe. The nuts (be sure to buy unsalted ones) provide a contrasting crunch, but must be added at the last minute or they'll turn soft.

Serves 4
180 Calories a portion

UK	**US**
4 leeks	4 leeks
225g/8 oz button mushrooms	8 ounces button mushrooms
1 orange	1 orange
2 tablespoons sunflower oil	2 tablespoons sunflower oil
50g/2 oz unsalted cashew nuts	½ cup unsalted cashew nuts

1. Trim leeks, slice diagonally, wash thoroughly and pat dry with kitchen towel. Wipe and halve mushrooms and squeeze juice from orange.
2. Heat the oil in a large non-stick frying pan (skillet), add the nuts and stir-fry, tossing continuously, until golden. Remove nuts from pan and drain on a piece of kitchen towel.
3. Add the leeks to the pan and stir-fry for 3–4 minutes until just softened.
4. Add the mushrooms and orange juice. Stir together over a high heat to reduce the liquid to a syrupy consistency. Scatter over the nuts and serve immediately.

Not suitable for freezing.

Tomato and Mushroom Potpourri_____

I called this recipe 'potpourri' because a fragrant mixture of herbs and spices are used for its flavouring. It's very quick to prepare and nice and juicy to serve with anything grilled or baked.

Serves 4
100 Calories a portion

UK

4 large tomatoes
1 teaspoon coriander seeds
2 tablespoons olive oil
1 bay leaf
1 sprig of fresh thyme or ¼ teaspoon
   dried
100ml/4 fl oz dry white wine
1 fat clove garlic
225g/8 oz button mushrooms
freshly ground black pepper
fresh parsley, to garnish

US

4 large tomatoes
1 teaspoon coriander seeds
2 tablespoons olive oil
1 bay leaf
1 sprig of fresh thyme or ¼ teaspoon
   dried
½ cup dry white wine
1 fat clove garlic
8 ounces button mushrooms
freshly ground black pepper
fresh parsley, to garnish

1. Roughly chop tomatoes. Crush coriander seeds. If you haven't a pestle and mortar, grind using the end of a wooden rolling pin in a strong bowl.
2. Heat the oil in a small saucepan and gently sweat the tomatoes with the coriander seeds, bay leaf and thyme until the tomatoes have softened and cooked down slightly.
3. Add the wine, and crush in the garlic and cook gently for a further 5 minutes, until the wine has reduced by half.
4. Meanwhile, trim and halve mushrooms. Add to the pan, season with pepper, cover and cook very gently for 2–3 minutes until just softened.
5. Chop a little parsley. Serve as soon as the mushrooms are cooked, sprinkled with parsley.

Not suitable for freezing.

Baked Courgette and Tomato Layer

Try to use really tasty tomatoes for this dish — so often they can lack flavour. Homegrown varieties are at their best in the late summer or look out for the flavourful plum tomatoes.

Serves 4
60 Calories a portion

UK	US
3–4 courgettes	3–4 zucchini
4 large tomatoes	4 large tomatoes
1 tablespoon olive oil	1 tablespoon olive oil
freshly ground black pepper	freshly ground black pepper
1 orange	1 orange
1 clove garlic	1 clove garlic
sprigs of fresh thyme or ½ teaspoon dried	sprigs of fresh thyme or ½ teaspoon dried

1. Trim the ends of the courgettes (zucchini) then slice diagonally — they look more attractive this way than sliced straight across in rounds. Slice the tomatoes.
2. Brush the oil over the bottom of an ovenproof dish. Layer the courgettes and tomatoes in the dish, sprinkling plenty of pepper over the layers as you go along.
3. Grate the rind from the orange and squeeze the juice from one half (you can squeeze and drink the other half!).
4. Add the rind to the juice and crush in the garlic and dried thyme if using. Pour over the courgettes (zucchini) and tomatoes and scatter the fresh thyme over the top.
5. Cover and bake at 200°C/400°F/Gas Mark 6 for 45 minutes until the courgettes are tender.

May be frozen. Use within 3 months.
Thaw overnight in the refrigerator, then reheat gently in a covered dish in a moderate oven.

Leek and Potato Cakes

Delicious as an accompaniment to a casserole, this is a mixture of leeks, mashed potato and watercress with a topping of sliced tomatoes.

Serves 4–6
275–185 Calories a portion

UK

900g/2 lb potatoes
2–3 leeks
2–3 tomatoes
bunch of watercress
25g/1 oz polyunsaturated margarine
freshly ground black pepper

US

2 pounds potatoes
2–3 leeks
2–3 tomatoes
bunch of watercress
2½ tablespoons polyunsaturated
   margarine
freshly ground black pepper

1. Peel the potatoes, cut into cubes and cook in boiling water until tender.
2. Slice and wash leeks. Slice tomatoes. Chop watercress.
3. Place leeks in a large non-stick frying pan (skillet) with the margarine and sweat until soft.
4. Drain and mash potatoes with some of their cooking water. Mix in leeks and watercress.
5. Pile mixture into a lightly–greased ovenproof dish and smooth down. Arrange tomatoes over the top, grind over some pepper, then pop under the grill (broiler) for about 5 minutes to finish off.
6. Serve cut into wedges.

Not suitable for freezing.

Spicy Red Cabbage With Apples_____

Full of fruit and spice flavours, this dish is delicious served with cold meat or poultry.

Serves 6
115 Calories a portion

UK	**US**
450g/1 lb red cabbage	1 pound red cabbage
2 onions	2 onions
2 cooking apples	2 cooking apples
50g/2 oz sultanas	⅓ cup golden seedless raisins
small piece fresh root ginger	small piece fresh root ginger
¼ teaspoon ground cinnamon	¼ teaspoon ground cinnamon
3 cloves	3 cloves
2 tablespoons brown sugar	2 tablespoons brown sugar
150ml/¼ pint unsweetened apple juice	⅔ cup unsweetened apple juice
2 tablespoons cider vinegar	2 tablespoons cider vinegar
1 clove garlic	1 clove garlic
freshly ground black pepper	freshly ground black pepper
15g/½ oz polyunsaturated margarine	1 tablespoon polyunsaturated margarine

1. Shred the cabbage finely, slice the onions and peel, core and slice the apples.
2. Layer the cabbage, onion, apple and sultanas (golden seedless raisins) in a large flameproof casserole (Dutch oven).
3. Peel and finely chop ginger. Add the ginger, cinnamon, cloves and sugar to the apple juice and vinegar in a jug. Crush in the garlic and season with pepper. Pour into the casserole and add margarine.
4. Cover with a tight-fitting lid and cook gently for 45 minutes to 1 hour until tender.

Not suitable for freezing.

Courgettes and Carrot Batons With Lemon_

The contrasting colours of these two vegetables look wonderful and taste scrumptious tossed together in lemon, honey and parsley. Chunky sticks take no longer to prepare than ordinary round slices yet have so much more appeal.

Serves 4
50 Calories a portion

UK

4 medium carrots
2–3 courgettes
1 lemon
few sprigs parsley (or other fresh herb, like thyme)
15g/½ oz polyunsaturated margarine
1 teaspoon clear honey
freshly ground black pepper

US

4 medium carrots
2–3 zucchini
1 lemon
few sprigs parsley (or other fresh herb, like thyme)
1 tablespoon polyunsaturated margarine
1 teaspoon clear honey
freshly ground black pepper

1. Peel carrots then top-and-tail both carrots and courgettes. Cut vegetables into chunky sticks about 3 in (7.5 cm) long.
2, Either steam vegetables or cook them in a very little boiling water until just tender but still firm. Drain.
3. Grate rind from lemon and squeeze juice. Chop some parsley to give about 2 tablespoons.
4. Place lemon rind and juice, margarine and honey in saucepan with vegetables, toss together and warm through. Grind over some pepper and serve sprinkled with parsley.

Not suitable for freezing.

Carrot and Bean Podial

This recipe comes from the Bombay Brasserie in London (opposite Gloucester Road underground station, SW7), one of the best modern-style Indian restaurants, where I once had the opportunity to meet the chef and discuss his delicious dishes. This makes an unusual accompaniment to anything spicy.

Serves 4
130 Calories a portion

UK

100g/4 oz carrots
100g/4 oz French beans
small piece of fresh root ginger
1 small chilli
2 tablespoons sunflower oil
2 teaspoons mustard seeds
50g/2 oz unsweetened flaked coconut

US

4 ounces carrots
4 ounces French beans
small piece of fresh root ginger
1 small green chilli pepper
2 tablespoons sunflower oil
2 teaspoons mustard seeds
½ cup unsweetened flaked coconut

1. Peel carrots and cut into sticks. Top, tail and halve beans. Peel and finely chop ginger. Deseed and chop chilli, taking care not to touch your eyes whilst preparing as it will sting.
2. Blanch carrots and beans in boiling water for 5 minutes, then drain and put to one side.
3. Heat oil in a frying pan (skillet) then add the mustard seeds and coconut. Fry gently for about 3 minutes.
4. Add the vegetables, ginger and chilli, stir over the heat for a few minutes, then serve.

Not suitable for freezing.

Spicy New Potatoes With French Beans————

Two summer vegetables tossed in a hot cumin, coriander and mustard seed dressing.

Serves 4
180 Calories a portion

UK	**US**
450g/1 lb new potatoes	1 pound new potatoes
225g/8 oz French beans	8 ounces snap beans
1 teaspoon coriander seeds	1 teaspoon coriander seeds
1 teaspoon cumin seeds	1 teaspoon cumin seeds
1 teaspoon mustard seeds	1 teaspoon mustard seeds
2 tablespoons olive oil	2 tablespoons olive oil
2 teaspoons wine vinegar	2 teaspoons wine vinegar

1. Scrub the potatoes and halve. Top–and–tail beans and halve.
2. Cook the vegetables in boiling water until tender.
3. Crush the coriander, cumin and mustard seeds, using a pestle and mortar or a coffee grinder.
4. Heat the oil and vinegar in a pan and add the spices. Cook lightly for 30 seconds.
5. Drain the vegetables, toss in the hot dressing, then serve immediately.

Not suitable for freezing.

Potato and Parsnip Puree

All root vegetables go well together. This combination makes a delicious winter vegetable accompaniment to grilled meat.

Serves 4
155 Calories a portion

UK

450g/1 lb potatoes
450g/1 lb parsnips
1 orange
2–3 tablespoons natural low-fat yogurt
1 teaspoon ground cinnamon
freshly ground black pepper

US

1 pound potatoes
1 pound parsnips
1 orange
2–3 tablespoons plain low-fat yogurt
1 teaspoon ground cinnamon
freshly ground black pepper

1. Peel the potatoes and parsnips, then cut into chunks. Cook in boiling water in a covered pan for about 20 minutes until tender.
2. Grate rind from orange. Drain potatoes and parsnips and mash with yogurt, cinnamon and orange rind. Season to taste with pepper.

Not suitable for freezing.

Baked Garlic Potatoes

These are prepared rather like garlic bread, basted in their skins with garlic–and–parsley–
-flavoured oil, then wrapped in foil and baked in the oven.

Serves 4
160 Calories a portion

UK

4 medium potatoes
2–3 cloves garlic
2 tablespoons sunflower oil
small bunch of parsley
freshly ground black pepper

US

4 medium potatoes
2–3 cloves garlic
2 tablespoons sunflower oil
small bunch of parsley
freshly ground black pepper

1. Wash potatoes (do not peel) then cut slices across at 5mm (¼ in) intervals, almost through, but keeping each potato whole.
2. Crush the garlic into the oil. Finely chop parsley and add about 1 heaped tablespoon to the oil. Season with pepper.
3. Place each potato on a small square of foil. Brush with oil mixture, making sure it goes inside the slices, then enclose in the foil.
4. Place on a baking tray and bake at 200°C/400°F/Gas Mark 6 for 1 hour or until soft. Unwrap foil and serve.

Not suitable for freezing.

Spiced Pilau Rice

Fragrant with spices and subtly coloured with saffron, this makes the perfect accompaniment to curries and anything spicy. For the authentic dish, basmati rice should be used, but for higher fibre value, brown rice tastes just as good.

Serves 4–6   265–175 Calories a portion

UK	**US**
1 small onion, finely chopped	1 small onion, finely chopped
2 tablespoons sunflower oil	2 tablespoons sunflower oil
pinch of saffron threads	pinch of saffron threads
4 cardamom pods	4 cardamom pods
1 teaspoon cumin seeds	1 teaspoon cumin seeds
2.5cm/1 in cinnamon stick	1 inch cinnamon stick
4 cloves	4 cloves
1 bay leaf	1 bay leaf
225g/8 oz basmati or brown rice	1 cup basmati or brown rice
600–750ml/1–1¼ pints vegetable stock	2½–3 cups vegetable stock

1. Heat oil in a heavy-based pan, add the onion and fry gently until softened.
2. Put saffron in a cup, add a couple of tablespoons of boiling water and leave to soak.
3. Shell cardamom pods, then crush the seeds with the cumin. Add to the onion with the cinnamon, cloves and bay leaf, stir and heat for a couple of minutes to draw out the fragrance of the spices.
4. Rinse rice thoroughly in a sieve (wire mesh colander) under running water until the water runs clear and the excess starch is removed. Drain the rice. Add the rice to the pan, stirring it around so it is coated with oil.
5. Pour in stock, using larger quantity for brown rice, plus the saffron liquid, cover with a tight-fitting lid and simmer gently for 15 minutes (30–40 minutes for brown rice) until the rice is tender. Check towards the end of the cooking time that it doesn't need a little more stock. When cooked the rice should be just tender and all the liquid should be absorbed. Tip into a serving dish and fluff up with a fork.

> Thaw overnight in the refrigerator, then reheat in a covered dish in a moderate oven.   May be frozen. Use within 6 months.

Orange and Cinnamon Rice

Why settle for plain boiled rice when it's so easy to add a few simple flavourings? Cook rice by the absorption method so you don't throw away any flavour in the cooking water.

Serves 2–3   235–155 Calories a portion

UK

1 orange
100g/4 oz brown rice
about 350ml/12 fl oz vegetable stock or
    water
½ cinnamon stick

US

1 orange
½ cup brown rice
1½ cups vegetable stock or water
½ cinnamon stick

1. Grate the rind from the orange and squeeze the juice.
2. Rinse the rice in a sieve (wire mesh colander) under running water until the water runs clear and the excess starch is removed. Drain the rice and tip it into a saucepan. Add the stock, orange juice and rind and cinnamon. Bring to the boil, then turn down heat, cover with a tight-fitting lid, and cook gently for about 30–40 minutes, until the rice is tender. Add a little boiling water if necessary. When cooked, the rice should be just tender and all the liquid should be absorbed.

May be frozen, although it's hardly worth using up the freezer space since it takes as long to thaw and reheat as to cook from raw! Use within six months.

Coconut and Lemon Rice

Rice cooked in this unusual, delicious way goes well with spicy or stir-fried dishes. Use brown or basmati rice, both of which are far tastier than regular long grain rice.

Serves 4–6
315–210 Calories a portion

UK

225g/8 oz brown or basmati rice
1 lemon
about 600ml/1 pint vegetable stock or
  water
50g/2 oz creamed coconut

US

1 cup brown or basmati rice
1 lemon
about 2½ cups vegetable stock or water
¼ cup creamed coconut

1. First rinse the rice thoroughly in a sieve (wire mesh colander) under running water until the water runs clear and the excess starch is removed. Leave the rice to drain.
2. Grate the rind from the lemon and squeeze juice. Place rice in a large saucepan with the stock, coconut, lemon rind and juice and bring to the boil. Stir to dissolve coconut, then turn down heat, cover and cook gently. Basmati rice will take about 15 minutes, for brown rice allow 30–40 minutes. Add a little more boiling water if it seems necessary. When cooked, the rice should be just tender and all the liquid absorbed. Serve warm.

> May be frozen; although it is hardly worth using up the freezer space since it takes as long to thaw and reheat as to cook from raw! Use within 6 months.

Minty Potato Raita

This is a yogurt side dish, excellent served with spicy dishes. Indian restaurants generally make it with cucumber but personally I'm rather fond of this potato version, flavoured with onion and mint — if possible use fresh mint rather than dried.

Serves 2–3
145–95 Calories a portion

UK

225g/8 oz potato
2 spring onions
small bunch of fresh mint or 1 teaspoon
   dried
150ml/¼ pint natural low-fat yogurt
a little chilli powder

US

8 ounces potato
2 scallions (green onions
small bunch of fresh mint or 1 teaspoon
   dried
⅔ cup plain low-fat yogurt
a little chilli powder

1. Peel the potato and cut it into small cubes. Cook in boiling water, with some sprigs of fresh mint, if available, for about 5 minutes until just tender, then drain and allow to cool.
2. Trim and chop the onions (scallions). Finely chop about a tablespoon of fresh mint.
3. Stir the onions and mint into the yogurt, then fold in the potatoes. Turn into an attractive serving dish and sprinkle a little chilli powder over the top.

Not suitable for freezing.

LIGHT MEALS AND SALADS

Tabbouleh

This is a delicious Middle Eastern salad made with bulgur (cracked wheat) and fresh herbs tossed in a citrus dressing. I remember first tasting it many years ago in New York, where it's always available in salad bars and delicatessens. It is very easy to prepare and best made several hours before you need it. It is essential that, for the best flavour, you use fresh mint and parsley. There's no cooking required, just a short soaking in boiling water. It's a scrumptious addition to a salad meal.

Serves 6
150 Calories a portion

UK	US
150g/5 oz cracked bulgur wheat	1 scant cupful cracked bulgur wheat
300ml/½ pint boiling water	1¼ cups boiling water
1 lemon	1 lemon
3 tablespoons olive oil	3 tablespoons olive oil
1 clove garlic	1 clove garlic
freshly ground black pepper	freshly ground black pepper
3 spring onions	3 scallions (green onions)
2–3 tomatoes	2–3 tomatoes
½ green pepper	½ green bell pepper
50g/2 oz fresh parsley	2 cups fresh parsley
25g/1 oz fresh mint	1 cup fresh mint

1. Place wheat in a bowl, pour over boiling water and leave to soak for 30 minutes to soften. It should absorb all the water. If the water has not been absorbed, drain it through a sieve (colander) for a short time.

2. Meanwhile, grate lemon rind and squeeze juice and blend both with the oil in a jug. Crush in the garlic and season with plenty of pepper.
3. Chop spring onions (scallions) and tomatoes and deseed and dice the pepper. Finely chop parsley and mint, in a food processor if you have one.
4. Stir together the soaked bulgur, onions, tomatoes, pepper, herbs and dressing in a serving bowl, then cover and chill for several hours. You can garnish it with twists of lemon and sprigs of mint.

Not suitable for freezing.

103

Big Munch Salad

A crisp, colourful salad packed with vitamins. Any other types of sprouts can be substituted, such as chick-pea, soya, alfalfa or fenugreek. Pour over dressing just before serving.

Serves 2
590 Calories a portion

UK

100g/4 oz bean sprouts
1 carton mustard and cress
2 carrots
¼ cucumber
1 kiwi fruit
1 large orange
75g/3 oz walnut halves
25g/1 oz pumpkin seeds

DRESSING:

3 tablespoons olive oil
1 tablespoon raspberry or cider vinegar
juice of ½ orange
1 tablespoon cranberry sauce
freshly ground black pepper

US

2 cups bean sprouts
1 carton mustard and cress
2 carrots
¼ cucumber
1 kiwi fruit
1 large orange
¾ cup walnut halves
¼ cup pumpkin seeds

DRESSING:

3 tablespoons olive oil
1 tablespoon raspberry or cider vinegar
juice of ½ orange
1 tablespoon cranberry sauce
freshly ground black pepper

1. Rinse the bean sprouts in a sieve (colander) under running water and trim the earthy roots off the cress.
2. Peel off the outside of the carrots and discard, then continue peeling to make carrot strips. Cut the cucumber lengthways into fine julienne sticks about 5 cm/2 in long.
3. Peel kiwi fruit and cut into wedges. Cut peel and pith from orange and cut fruit into segments, removing any pips.
4. Place all the salad ingredients, including the walnuts and pumpkin seeds, in a large

bowl and all the dressing ingredients in a screw-top jar. When ready to eat, shake the dressing, pour over the salad and toss together.

Not suitable for freezing.

Carrot Salad With Mint and Cumin

Grated carrot is mixed with two interesting flavours to make a really intriguing tasting side salad. The thinly–sliced radish makes a pretty colour contrast to the orange of the carrots. If you can, it is better to use fresh mint rather than dried mint in the salad.

Serves 4
105 Calories a portion

UK

4 large carrots
6 radishes
3 tablespoons olive oil
1 tablespoon lemon juice
½ teaspoon ground cumin
½ teaspoon wholegrain mustard
small bunch of fresh mint or ½ teaspoon
   dried
freshly ground black pepper
sprigs of fresh mint to garnish

US

4 large carrots
6 radishes
3 tablespoons olive oil
1 tablespoon lemon juice
½ teaspoon ground cumin
½ teaspoon wholegrain mustard
small bunch of fresh mint or ½ teaspoon
   dried
freshly ground black pepper
sprigs of fresh mint to garnish

1. Peel carrots, then coarsely grate into a bowl. Trim radishes, then slice thinly and add to the carrots.
2. Whisk together the oil, lemon juice, cumin and mustard. Chop about 1 tablespoon fresh mint and add this or the dried mint to the dressing. Season with pepper, pour over carrots and toss. Garnish with sprigs of fresh mint, if available.

Not suitable for freezing.

Turkey and Avocado Salad With Strawberries

A summery main-meal salad with a light strawberry dressing. It looks very pretty and would make a nice choice for an informal lunch. The turkey can be cooked and the dressing made ahead of time, but it should only be assembled shortly before serving.

Serves 4
420 Calories a portion

UK	US
DRESSING:	DRESSING:
50g/2 oz strawberries	½ cup strawberries
4 tablespoons olive oil	5 tablespoons olive oil
1–2 teaspoons lemon juice	1–2 teaspoons lemon juice
freshly ground black pepper	freshly ground black pepper
pinch of sugar	pinch of sugar
SALAD:	SALAD:
450g/1 lb cooked turkey	1 pound cooked turkey
225g/8 oz strawberries	8 ounces strawberries
1 large avocado	1 large avocado
juice of ½ lemon	juice of ½ lemon
1 head of frisée (curly endive)	1 head of chicory
1 bunch of watercress	1 bunch of watercress

1. First make the dressing. Hull the strawberries, then purée in a blender or food processor. Gradually blend in the oil, then add lemon juice, pepper and a little sugar to taste.

2. Remove any skin from turkey, then slice into neat pieces. Hull and halve the strawberries. Halve avocado, remove stone and scoop into balls, using a melon baller. Alternatively, slice avocado. Squeeze over a little lemon juice to prevent it discolouring.

3. Break off a number of nice frisée (chicory) leaves, trim ends, rinse and dry. Arrange around the edge of your serving dish. Trim and rinse watercress.
4. Combine the turkey, strawberries, avocado and watercress in a large bowl. Drizzle over the dressing, toss lightly, then spoon the mixture into the centre of the serving dish. Serve immediately.

Not suitable for freezing.

Beans Galore Salad

Any selection of beans can be used for this nourishing salad, but for salt-free diets, it's best not to use the canned varieties as they are packed in brine. Packets of mixed dried varieties are handy. A favourite of mine contains chick-peas and haricot, black-eyed, kidney, pinto and soya beans.

Serves 8
150 Calories a portion

UK

SALAD:

225g/8 oz mixed dried beans
1 small onion
3-4 cloves
1 bay leaf
1 clove garlic
few sprigs fresh thyme or parsley
225g/8 oz fresh green beans, such as
    French or dwarf
3-4 spring onions (or 1 red onion)
small bunch fresh coriander or parsley

DRESSING:

4 tablespoons olive oil
1 tablespoon red wine vinegar
1 teaspoon wholegrain mustard
1 clove garlic
freshly ground black pepper

US

SALAD:

1 cup mixed dried beans
1 small onion
3-4 cloves
1 bay leaf
1 clove garlic
few sprigs fresh thyme or parsley
8 ounces snap beans
3-4 scallions (green onions) (or 1 red
    onion)
small bunch cilantro or parsley

DRESSING:

5 tablespoons olive oil
1 tablespoon red wine vinegar
1 teaspoon wholegrain mustard
1 clove garlic
freshly ground black pepper

1. Soak dried beans overnight in plenty of cold water.
2. Drain and rinse beans, then place in a large pan with fresh cold water. Bring to the boil and boil rapidly for 10 minutes. Spoon off any scum on the surface and add the

onion, studded with the cloves, the bay leaf, crushed garlic and sprigs of thyme or parsley. Reduce heat, cover and simmer for 45 minutes.

3. Top-and-tail green beans are cut crossways into three. Add to the pan and cook for a further 10 minutes, until all the beans and tender.

4. Meanwhile, make the dressing. Measure the oil, vinegar and mustard into a screw-top jar, crush in the garlic and season with pepper.

5. Drain beans, discarding the onion, bay leaf and herbs. Place in a serving dish, shake the dressing and pour over while the beans are still warm — they will take up the flavour of the dressing better.

6. Slice spring onions (scallions). Finely chop the coriander (cilantro) or parsley — this is easy to do if placed in a mug and snipped with sharp scissors. Add onions and coriander to beans and toss thoroughly.

Not suitable for freezing.

Double Cabbage Slaw

A coleslaw variation using two types of cabbage, red and the traditional white. Red cabbage is sometimes cooked with apple and caraway seeds — both are equally good added to a cabbage salad. This makes an excellent winter salad, especially useful for buffets. It is also an inexpensive dish at a time when many other salad ingredients are quite pricey or unavailable.

Serves 6–8
110–80 Calories a portion

UK

DRESSING:

4 tablespoons olive oil
1 tablespoon cider vinegar
1 teaspoon honey
1 teaspoon caraway seeds
freshly ground black pepper

SALAD:

2 dessert apples
juice of 1 lemon
¼ small white cabbage
¼ small red cabbage

US

DRESSING:

5 tablespoons olive oil
1 tablespoon cider vinegar
1 teaspoon honey
1 teaspoon caraway seeds
freshly ground black pepper

SALAD:

2 dessert apples
juice of 1 lemon
¼ small white cabbage
¼ small red cabbage

1. Measure all the dressing ingredients into a screw-top jar.
2. Core the apples, then slice wafer-thin and toss in the lemon juice, to prevent them browning.
3. Shred both the cabbages (this only takes seconds in a food processor if you have one). Toss cabbage and apples together in a large salad bowl.
4. Shake the dressing in the jar, pour over the salad and toss well.

Not suitable for freezing.

Pasta With Nuts and Garlic

Quick and delicious any you can use any shape of pasta you fancy from ordinary spaghetti to fancy spirals (fusilli) or bows (farfelle). Serve as a light meal with a fresh salad.

Serves 4
385 Calories a portion

UK

225g/ 8 oz wholewheat pasta
2 cloves garlic
50g/2 oz walnuts
4 tablespoons olive oil
1 lemon
fresh parsley
freshly ground black pepper

US

2 cups wholewheat pasta
2 cloves garlic
½ cup walnuts
5 tablespoons olive oil
1 lemon
fresh parsley
freshly ground black pepper

1. Cook pasta in a large pan of boiling water for about 10 minutes (depending on shape, follow instructions on pack) until *al dente*, slightly firm to the bite.
2. Meanwhile, crush garlic and chop walnuts and place in another pan with the oil, Sauté gently for a few minutes, then turn off heat.
3. Grate lemon rind and squeeze juice and add to garlicky oil. Finely chop about 2 tablespoons parsley and add.
4. Drain pasta, stir in oil mixture, season with plenty of pepper and serve immediately.

Not suitable for freezing.

Fruit-and-Vegetable Risotto

A colourful medley of ingredients which can be varied in so many ways to suit whatever you have in the refrigerator and store cupboard. A dish which is useful for when there's no time to shop. If you happen to have a bottle of white wine open, substitute it for some of the stock to give extra flavour.

Serves 4
335 Calories a portion

UK

1 onion
1 clove garlic
1 tablespoon sunflower oil
225g/8 oz brown rice
850ml/1½ pints vegetable stock
1 teaspoon dried thyme
grated rind of 1 lemon
220g/8 oz can pineapple in fruit juice
50g/2 oz sultanas
1 red pepper
100g/4 oz frozen peas
freshly ground black pepper
fresh parsley
50g/2 oz unsalted cashew nuts

US

1 onion
1 clove garlic
1 tablespoon sunflower oil
1 cup brown rice
3¾ cups vegetable stock
1 teaspoon dried thyme
grated rind of 1 lemon
8 ounce can pineapple in fruit juice
⅓ cup golden seedless raisins
1 red bell pepper
1 cup frozen peas
freshly ground black pepper
fresh parsley
½ cup unsalted cashew nuts

1. Slice the onion and crush the garlic. Heat the oil in a large heavy-based pan and cook the onion gently until soft. Add the garlic and cook for a further minute.
2. Stir in the rice, then pour in the stock (including wine if using) and add the thyme, lemon rind, drained juice from the pineapple and sultanas (golden seedless raisins). Cover and cook gently for 20 minutes.
3. Chop and deseed the pepper and add to the rice with the peas. Cover and cook for a further 10–15 minutes until the rice is tender. Add a little more stock if necessary but all the liquid should be absorbed by the time the risotto is cooked.

4. Meanwhile, chop about 2 tablespoons parsley and toast the cashews on a baking sheet under the grill (broiler)
5. Season risotto with pepper to taste, stir in the parsley and serve scattered with cashew nuts.

> May be frozen. Use within 2 months.
> Thaw overnight in the refrigerator, then reheat gently in a covered dish in the oven until thoroughly heated through.

Courgette (Zucchini) and Mushroom Omelette

A substantial vegetable filling, flavoured with garlic and tarragon. Tarragon has a great natural affinity with eggs and most vegetables, but is particularly good with courgettes (zucchini). Always use fresh herbs, if possible.

Serves 4   195 Calories a portion

UK

2 medium courgettes
100g/4 oz mushrooms
50g/2 oz polyunsaturated margarine
1 fat clove garlic
2 teaspoons fresh or 1 teaspoon dried
    tarragon
freshly ground black pepper
4 fresh eggs

US

2 medium zucchini
4 ounces mushrooms
¼ cup polyunsaturated margarine
1 fat clove garlic
2 teaspoons fresh or 1 teaspoon dried
    tarragon
freshly ground black pepper
4 fresh eggs

1. Top and tail the courgettes (zucchini) then grate them, leaving the skin on. The grating disc on a food processor does this job in seconds.
2. Trim the mushrooms, then roughly chop them.
3. Melt half the margarine in a small pan, add the mushrooms, crush in the garlic and add tarragon. Sauté gently for just a couple of minutes until the mushrooms are softened. Stir in the courgettes. Season with pepper and cook for just 1 minute so they are no more than slightly cooked. Take off heat but cover to keep warm.
4. Making one omelette at a time, beat each egg with 1 tablespoon of water and some pepper, then cook in an omelette pan (small skillet) with a knob of the remaining margarine until set underneath. Spoon a quarter of the vegetable mixture over half the omelette. Cook for about 30 seconds, then fold the other half of the omelette over the filling and turn it out of the pan on to the plate.

Not suitable for freezing.

Piperade

This is a Provençal dish of eggs and Mediterranean vegetables. It can be cooked either as scrambled eggs and eaten immediately, or as an omelette, served cut into wedges and eaten hot or cold.

Serves 4   165 Calories a portion

UK

1 medium onion
2 peppers (preferably 1 red and 1 green)
1 clove garlic
4 tomatoes
2 tablespoons olive oil
freshly ground black pepper
4 eggs

US

1 medium onion
2 bell peppers
1 clove garlic
4 tomatoes
2–3 tablespoons olive oil
freshly ground black pepper
4 eggs

1. Chop onion. Deseed peppers and slice into thin strips. Crush garlic. Skin and chop tomatoes. (To skin tomatoes, place in a bowl and pour over boiling water to cover. Leave for about 30 seconds, then drain and pour over cold water. The skins should come away quite easily.)
2. Heat oil in a large frying pan (skillet) and sauté the onion first until soft. Then stir in the peppers, cook for a further 5 minutes. Stir in the tomatoes and garlic, season with pepper and cook for 5 minutes more.
3. Beat the eggs with 1 tablespoon of water then pour into the pan and cook on a low heat. You can either stir lightly to produce scrambled eggs or cook like an omelette.

Not suitable for freezing.

Herby Fish Cakes

White fish mixed with mashed potatoes and herbs, then shaped and coated with oats, nuts and seeds. If you wish, you can make them from left-over cooked potato and fish. Serve with a tomato and parsley salad or Tomato and Mushroom Potpourri (see page 89).

Serves 4 (Makes 8)
340 Calories a portion (170 Calories each)

UK

350g/12 oz potatoes
350g/12 oz white fish fillet (such as cod or haddock)
150ml/¼ pint skimmed milk
freshly ground black pepper
1 bay leaf
15g/½ oz polyunsaturated margarine
2–3 spring onions
small bunch of parsley
1 egg
50g/2 oz porridge oats
25g/ 1 oz chopped nuts (unsalted)
25g/1 oz sesame seeds

US

12 ounces potatoes
12 ounces white fish fillet
⅔ cup skim milk
freshly ground black pepper
1 bay leaf
1 tablespoon polyunsaturated margarine
2–3 scallions (green onions)
small bunch of parsley
1 egg
⅔ cup rolled oats
2 tablespoons chopped nuts (unsalted)
2 tablespoons sesame seeds

1. Peel and cube potatoes then cook in boiling water until tender.
2. Meanwhile, poach fish in milk seasoned with some pepper and a bay leaf for about 10 minutes, until tender.
3. Drain fish, reserving the milk. Flake the fish removing any skin and bones. Drain the potatoes and mash with half the milk from the fish, and the margarine.
4. Mix together the fish and potatoes. Trim and chop spring onions (scallions). Chop about 2 tablespoons parsley. Add both to fish mixture and season with plenty of pepper. If the mixture is still warm, chill before shaping.
5. Shape into 8 flat round cakes. Beat egg, then pour onto a plate. Mix together oats, nuts and seeds on another plate. Dip fish cakes first in egg, then oat mixture.

6. Place on a greased baking tray. Bake at 200°C/400°F Gas Mark 6 for about 30 minutes or grill on both sides until crisp and golden.

May be frozen. Use within 1 month.
Reheat from frozen in a moderate oven, until thoroughly heated through.

Mexican Picadillo

This is a savoury mince (ground meat) with almonds and raisins. It can be served inside wholewheat pitta breads or pancakes or used as a topping for baked jacket potatoes.

Serves 4   320 Calories a portion (without serving suggestion)

UK

1 onion
5–6 tomatoes
450g/1 lb lean minced beef, pork or
   turkey
1–2 cloves garlic
2 tablespoons tomato purée
1 stick or ½ teaspoon ground cinnamon
freshly ground black pepper
50g/2 oz raisins
50g/2 oz flaked almonds

US

1 onion
5–6 tomatoes
1 pound lean minced beef, pork or
   turkey
1–2 cloves garlic
2 tablespoons tomato paste
1 stick or ½ teaspoon ground cinnamon
freshly ground black pepper
⅓ cup raisins
½ cup slivered almonds

1. Chop onion and skin and chop tomatoes. (Put tomatoes first in boiling water for 30 seconds then into cold to loosen skins.)
2. Place the meat in a large frying pan (skillet) and cook, without adding any fat or oil, until lightly browned. Stir in the onion and crush in garlic and continue to cook until onion has softened.
3. Add the tomatoes, purée (paste), cinnamon and raisins and season with pepper. Cover and cook gently for about 20 minutes, adding a little water if necessary. Stir occasionally.
4. Meanwhile, toast the almonds on a baking sheet under the grill (broiler).
5. Remove cinnamon stick, if used, scatter over the almonds and serve. Some natural (plain) yogurt goes well with it and you could serve a green salad on the side.

May be frozen (without nuts). Use within 3 months
Thaw overnight in the refrigerator, then reheat in a covered dish in a moderate oven until thoroughly heated through.

DESSERTS

Pears in Lemon and Ginger Syrup

A simple yet delicious dessert. It's ideal for dinner parties, because it can be prepared well in advance and left in the refrigerator until well chilled.

Serves 4   125 Calories a glass

UK

1 lemon
1 piece stem ginger
150ml/¼ pint water
75g/3 oz sugar
1 teaspoon ginger syrup
4 nice-shaped pears

US

1 lemon
1 piece stem ginger
⅔ cup water
½ cup sugar
1 teaspoon ginger syrup
4 nice-shaped pears

1. Thinly peel the rind from the lemon and cut into julienne strips. Blanch strips in a pan of boiling water for 10 minutes then drain. Squeeze the lemon juice.
2. Finely chop the stem ginger.
3. Pour the water into a pan, add the sugar and heat gently until the sugar has dissolved. Boil for 1–2 minutes, then add the lemon juice and rind, chopped ginger and syrup.
4. Peel the pears, leaving on the stalks, then place them in the syrup, cover and poach gently for 15–20 minutes, until just tender.
5. Chill and serve with Greek strained yogurt, if liked.

Not suitable for freezing.

Rhubarb and Raspberry Compote_____

Rhubarb is a somewhat undervalued fruit (technically, it's a vegetable), generally used for pies, crumbles and fools. Early in the growing season the stalks are pink and tender and make a pretty compote combined with the rich red of raspberries. I like to keep a box of raspberries in the freezer — they add colour to many desserts.

Serves 4
50 Calories a portion

UK

450g/1 lb early (forced) rhubarb
50g/2 oz sugar
½–1 teaspoon rosewater (see note)
225g/8 oz frozen raspberries, thawed

US

1 pound early (forced) rhubarb
⅓ cup sugar
½–1 teaspoon rosewater (see note)
8 ounces frozen raspberries, thawed

1. Trim rhubarb, then cut into short lengths. Unlike maincrop rhubarb which has tougher stalks, it should not require peeling.
2. Place rhubarb in a saucepan with 4 tablespoons water and the sugar, cover and simmer gently for about 5 minutes until just tender. Do not allow fruit to boil or it will lose its shape.
3. Tip into an attractive glass serving dish, stir in the rosewater and allow to cool. Taste to check sweetnesss.
4. When cool, gently stir in raspberries. Serve chilled with Greek strained yogurt.

Not suitable for freezing.

COOK'S NOTE: Rosewater can be bought from chemists (drug stores) or ethnic stores. It should be triple-distilled with a very concentrated flavour, so you only need use a very little. Start with adding just ½ teaspoon, then more if if you get carried away with the intoxicating fragrance.

Blackberry Apples With Meringue Hats

This dessert is very quick and simple to make, but it looks spectacular — as if you've gone to a lot of trouble! You can either use fresh blackberries or, if they are not available, canned blackberries in natural juice make a good substitute.

Serves 4–5
255–185 Calories a portion

UK

4–5 even-sized cooking apples
225g/8 oz blackberries or 300g/10 oz can in fruit juice
25–50g/1–2 oz sugar
1–2 tablespoons cassis (optional)

MERINGUE TOPPING:

2 egg whites
100g/4 oz sugar
grated rind of ½ lemon

US

4–5 even-sized cooking apples
8 ounces blackberries or 10 ounce can in fruit juice
2–3 tablespoons sugar
1–2 tablespoons cassis (optional)

MERINGUE TOPPING:

2 egg whites
⅔ cup sugar
grated rind of ½ lemon

1. Core the apples and score the skin round the middle of each. Place in a shallow ovenproof dish.
2. If using canned blackberries, drain the juice and reserve. Blend the blackberries with the sugar, using just enough to sweeten the fruit. Stir in the cassis if using.
3. Spoon the blackberry mixture into the centre of the apples and spoon 4 tablespoons water or 4 tablespoons of reserved juice around them.
4. Bake at 200°C/400°F/Gas Mark 6 for about 35 mintues or until just soft.
5. Meanwhile make up the meringue mixture. Whisk the egg whites until stiff, then whisk in half the sugar. Whisk in remaining sugar and grated lemon rind. Spoon into a piping bag fitted with a star nozzle.
6. Strip off top half of apple skins and pipe meringue on top of each. Return to the oven for a further 10–15 minutes until the meringue is golden. Serve immediately.

Not suitable for freezing.

Oranges in Cardamom Syrup

This makes a wonderful winter dessert when oranges are at their best. Choose a sweet, juicy and preferably seedless variety, such as Navels. Cardamom is one of my favourite spices, so fragrant it transforms any dish in which it is used.

Serves 4-6
170-115 Calories a portion

UK	US
150ml/¼ pint water	⅔ cup water
100g/ 4 oz sugar	⅔ cup sugar
6 cardamom pods	6 cardamom pods
4 juicy oranges	4 juicy oranges

1. Place water and sugar in a saucepan and heat gently until the sugar has dissolved. Then boil rapidly for about 5 minutes until syrupy and golden. Remove from heat.
2. Remove cardamom pods and crush the seeds inside. Add seeds to syrup.
3. While syrup is cooling, cut the peel and pith away from the oranges, then cut across into thin slices, catching any juice in a bowl.
4. Lay oranges in a glass serving dish with any of the reserved juice, then pour over the cooled syrup. Cover and chill thoroughly, preferably overnight.

Not suitable for freezing.

Fragrant Fruit Brulée

A useful dessert because it can be made in advance and can be varied to use virtually any selection of fruits. It is topped with a mixture of low-fat 'cream' substitute and natural yogurt, which gives a light yet creamy-tasting result. When ever I make this dessert, people always ask for second helpings. It is very moreish!

Serves 4
205 Calories a portion

UK

220g /8 oz can pineapple chunks, in fruit juice
2 large firm bananas
3 ripe pears
about 4 cardamom pods (optional)
150ml/¼ pint low-fat Double 'cream'
150ml/¼ pint natural low-fat yogurt
2 tablespoons light soft brown sugar
2 tablespoons flaked almonds

US

8 ounce can pineapple chunks, in fruit juice
2 large firm bananas
3 ripe pears
about 4 cardamom pods (optional)
⅔ cup low-fat Double 'cream'
⅔ cup plain low-fat yogurt
2 tablespoons light soft brown sugar
2 tablespoons slivered almonds

1. Empty the can of pineapple, including the juice, into a shallow heatproof dish. Peel and slice the bananas and pears. Add to the pineapple stir around gently.
2. Remove cardamom pods, crush the seeds and add to fruit if liked.
3. Whip the 'cream' until thick then fold in the yogurt. Spoon over fruit to cover evenly and then chill.
4. Just before serving, sprinkle sugar and almonds over the topping, then place under a preheated grill (broiler) for a few minutes to caramelize the sugar and toast the almonds. Cool before serving.

Not suitable for freezing.

Strawberries With Raspberry and Passion Fruit Sauce

I like to serve the fresh soft fruits of summer very simply so that their wonderous flavours are not masked. This fruit sauce is a great favourite in our household.

Serves 4
70 Calories a portion

UK

450g /1 lb strawberries
225g/8 oz raspberries
1 passion fruit
25g/1 oz icing sugar

US

1 pound strawberries
8 ounces raspberries
1 passion fruit
2 tablespoons confectioners' sugar

1. Hull the strawberries and place in a pretty serving bowl.
2. Place the raspberries in a blender or food processor. Cut passion fruit in half, scoop out pulpy flesh and add to raspberries. Blend until smooth, then sieve to remove pips.
3. Sift sugar into purée and pour over strawberries. Stir gently, then chill before serving.

Not suitable for freezing.

Mixed Berry Condé

A quick and easy store-cupboard dessert made up of layers of creamy rice pudding and fruit. You can use any mixture of soft berries. Usually I prefer to make use of fresh fruits in season, but this is one dessert where the canned varieties provide the soft juiciness required. If using fresh berries, you'll need to stir in some red jam to give extra colour and sweetness. Currants will need to be gently cooked until softened.

Serves 4
190 Calories a portion

UK

2 tablespoons short grain rice
450ml/¾ pint skimmed milk
2 tablespoons sugar
1 lemon
300g/10½ oz can raspberries, in fruit juice
300g/10½ oz can blackberries, in fruit juice
1 tablespoon blackcurrant or raspberry liqueur (optional)
85ml/3 fl oz low-fat Double 'Cream'

US

2 tablespoons short grain rice
2 cups skim milk
2 tablespoons sugar
1 lemon
10½ ounce can raspberries, in fruit juice
10½ ounce can blackberries, in fruit juice
1 tablespoon blackcurrant or raspberry liqueur (optional)
⅓ cup low-fat Double 'Cream'

1. Put the rice in a pan with the milk and sugar. Grate in the rind from the lemon, then cook gently for about 30 minutes until the rice is tender and most of the milk absorbed. Leave to cool.
2. Drain the raspberries and blackberries, using the juice for a fruit salad or for stewing some other fruit. Stir the berries together and blend in the liqueur if using.
3. Lightly whip the 'cream' then stir into the rice.
4. Layer rice and fruit mixtures into tall stemmed glasses and chill before serving.

Not suitable for freezing.

Fruit Kebabs

Quick, simple and appealing. You can vary the selection of fruits as long as they are suitable for grilling (broiling) on skewers. These kebabs can be prepared in advance, but cook them just before serving.

Serves 4
155 Calories a portion

UK

1 lemon
1 orange
3 fresh peaches
½ fresh pineapple
2 firm bananas
25g/1 oz polyunsaturated margarine
1 tablespoon maple syrup

US

1 lemon
1 orange
3 fresh peaches
½ fresh pineapple
2 firm bananas
2½ tablespoon polyunsaturated
   margarine
1 tablespoon maple syrup

1. Squeeze the juice from the lemon. Grate the rind from the orange and squeeze the juice. Combine the two juices and the rind in a shallow dish. Then add the fruit as you prepare it.
2. Halve and stone peaches then cut fruit into large bite-sized pieces. Cut off pineapple skin, remove core and cut fruit into chunks. Slice bananas thickly. Spoon the juice over the fruit. Cover and chill until ready to cook.
3. Soak the bamboo skewers in water for 10 minutes before threading to prevent them from burning.
4. Thread fruit alternatively onto bamboo skewers, about 2 pieces of each fruit per skewer.
5. Melt the margarine with the syrup and brush over the fruit. Place skewers under a preheated grill (broiler) and cook for about 10 minutes, turning them frequently until lightly browned. Serve immediately.

Not suitable for freezing.

Cranberry and Apple Nutty Oat Crumble

The tartness of cranberries combines beautifully with apples and provides a colourful filling for a crisp crumble topping . Cranberries freeze well, so buy them when you can and keep in the freezer for a later treat.

Serves 6
390 Calories a portion

UK

FILLING:

3–4 cooking apples
340g/12 oz cranberries
1 orange
50g/2 oz brown sugar

TOPPING:

100g/4 oz wholemeal flour
100g/4 oz porridge oats
75g/ 3 oz brown sugar
50g/2 oz walnut pieces
40g/1½ oz polyunsaturated margarine

US

FILLING:

3–4 cooking apples
12 ounces fresh cranberries
1 orange
⅓ cup brown sugar

TOPPING:

1 cup wholemeal flour
1 cup rolled oats
½ cup brown sugar
½ cup walnuts
4 tablespoons polyunsaturated margarine

1. Peel, core and slice the apples. Place in an oven proof dish with the cranberries. Grate rind from orange and squeeze juice. Stir rind and juice into fruit with the sugar and 2 tablespoons water.
2. For the topping, stir together the flour, oats and sugar. Roughly chop nuts and add. Melt margarine and stir in until all the ingredients are thoroughly blended.
3. Bake at 190°C/375°F/Gas Mark 5 for about 30 minutes until topping is lightly golden. Serve with natural (plain) yogurt.

> May be frozen. Use within 6 months.
> Thaw overnight in the refrigerator. Cover and reheat in a moderate oven.

Indian Rice Dessert

This is a recipe for Kheer, an Indian rice pudding fragrantly scented with cardamoms and rose water and finished with a scattering of nuts. The flavourings transform what is essentially an ordinary milk pudding into something rather special. Although it can be served warm, I think it is much nicer served cold. It goes well with exotic fruit, such as lychees, mangoes, figs or guavas.

Serves 4–6
285–190 Calories a portion

UK	US
50g/2 oz basmati rice	5 tablespoons basmati rice
1.1 litres/2 pints semi-skimmed milk	5 cups low-fat milk
50g/2 oz sugar	⅓ cup sugar
3 cardamom pods	3 cardamom pods
1 scant teaspoon rose water	1 scant teaspoon rose water
25g/1 oz unsalted pistachio nuts	3 tablespoons unsalted pistachio nuts

1. Rinse rice thoroughly in a sieve (wire mesh colander) under running water until the water runs clear and the excess starch is removed. Drain well.
2. Place the rice and milk in a heavy-based pan, bring to the boil, then turn down heat, and simmer very gently for about 1½ hours until the rice is soft.
3. Stir in sugar and cook for a further 5 minutes.
4. Remove pan from heat. Remove cardamom pods and crush the seeds. Stir seeds and the rose water into the rice and leave to cool. Then chill.
5. Just before serving, cut pistachios into thin slivers and scatter over the top.

Not suitable for freezing.

Harmonious Fruit Salad

To my mind, there's nothing to beat a really fresh fruit salad, using thoughtfully selected fruits with colours that will complement each other. So choose a colour scheme — red with orange, or green with yellow work well — and look out for exotic fruits as well as the more common ones.

Serves 4–6
75–50 Calories a portion

UK

100ml/4 fl oz unsweetened apple or
    grape juice
1 passion fruit
½ melon
2 kiwi fruit
100g/4 oz seedless grapes
½ pineapple

US

½ cup unsweetened apple or grape juice
1 passion fruit
½ melon
2 kiwi fruit
4 ounces seedless grapes
½ pineapple

1. Pour the juice into an attractive serving dish, then add the fruit as you prepare it.
2. Cut passion fruit in half and scoop out the pulpy flesh into the juice. Stir around.
3. Remove melon pips (seeds) and scoop out fruit using a melon baller or simply cut into small cubes.
4. Peel kiwi fruit and cut into segments or slices. Halve grapes. Cut off pineapple skin and cut flesh into small wedges. When all the fruit is in the bowl, stir around then cover and chill until ready to serve.

Not suitable for freezing.

Tropical Fruit Salad

This sophisticated dessert, enhanced by rum, is served in a pineapple shell. This combination of fruit from far-away places blends well and makes it very colourful. A very good choice for a special dinner party, since it looks spectacular served in the pineapple shells.

Serves 6
125 Calories a portion

UK	US
1 pineapple	1 pineapple
1 papaya (pawpaw)	1 papaya
1 mango	1 mango
1 lemon	1 lemon
2 bananas	2 bananas
2 juicy oranges	2 juicy oranges
2 tablespoons dark rum	2 tablespoons dark rum
15 g/½ oz unsweetened flaked coconut, to garnish	1–2 tablespoons unsweetened flaked coconut, to garnish

1. Cut pineapple in half lengthways, through the leaves. You will use both halves for serving the salad in. Using a sharp knife, cut round the inside of the skin and remove the fruit. Cut away core and cut fruit into neat wedges.
2. Peel the papaya, cut it in half and scoop out the seeds. Then cut flesh into neat pieces. Peel mango, cut flesh away from central stone, then slice.
3. Squeeze the juice from the lemon into a bowl and slice the bananas into it. Spoon the juice over the banana slices.
4. Squeeze the juice from the oranges and stir in rum.
5. Combine in a bowl all the fruit, lemon juice and orange and rum mixture. Cover and chill.
6. Just before serving, toast coconut on a baking sheet under the grill (broiler). Spoon fruit salad into pineapple shells and scatter coconut over the top.

Not suitable for freezing.

Baked Fruit Compote

This delicious combination of fresh apricots and dried dates, gently baked in the oven, then with the addition of some sliced bananas, is very good served warm with yogurt or fromage frais.

Serves 4
130 Calories a portion

UK

450g/1 lb fresh apricots
12 dried dates
2 oranges
1 cinnamon stick
2 large, firm bananas

US

1 pound fresh apricots
12 dried dates
2 oranges
1 cinnamon stick
2 large, firm bananas

1. Place the apricots in a heatproof dish with the dates. Squeeze the juice from the oranges and pour over. Add cinnamon stick. Cover and bake at 150°C/300°F/Gas Mark 2 for about 30 minutes or until the apricots are tender.
2. Remove from oven and slice in the bananas. Return to the oven for a further 5 minutes, just to lightly soften the bananas. Serve warm.

Not suitable for freezing.

Annie's Plombières

This recipe is dedicated to our very good friend, Annie Logan. She always described it as a thickened egg custard, lightened with egg whites, then with fresh fruits folded in. This is my version of it. It originates from the town of Plombières in France.

Serves 6
175 Calories a portion

UK

3 fresh eggs
25g/1 oz cornflour
50g/2 oz caster sugar
450ml/¾ pint semi-skimmed milk
2 large bananas
2–3 ripe peaches
225g/8 oz strawberries

US

3 fresh eggs
3 tablespoons cornstarch
⅓ cup superfine sugar
2 cups low-fat milk
2 large bananas
2–3 ripe peaches
8 ounces strawberries

1. Separate the eggs. Blend the egg yolks with the cornflour (cornstarch), sugar and 1 tablespoon of the milk. Heat the rest of the milk until just boiling. Stir into egg yolk mixture, then return to pan and heat, stirring continuously, until thickened. (It will be pretty thick, at this stage) Remove from heat, pour into a glass serving bowl and leave to cool.
2. Prepare all the fruit, slicing the bananas and peaches and halving any large strawberries. Stir fruit into cooled custard.
3. Whisk the egg whites until softly stiff, then gently fold into fruit custard. Cover and chill.

Not suitable for freezing.

Lychee and Ginger Sorbet

A light and refreshing water ice with a wonderfully fragrant flavour. This is one occasion when you need to use fruit canned in syrup since the sugar is essential to the recipe. Moreover, canned lychees seem to have a far more perfumed flavour than the fresh fruit. The ginger can be omitted if preferred.

Serves 6
75 Calories a portion

UK

565g/1 lb 4 oz can lychees in syrup
2 tabespoons lemon juice
1 piece stem ginger in syrup
1 teaspoon ginger syrup
1 egg white

US

20 ounce can lychees in syrup
2 tabespoons lemon juice
1 piece stem ginger in syrup
1 teaspoon ginger syrup
1 egg white

1. Tip the can of lychees, including the syrup into a food processor or blender. Add the lemon juice. Finely chop the ginger and add with the ginger syrup. Blend together.
2. Work the mixture through a sieve (a wire mesh colander) to make a smooth purée.
3. Pour into a shallow freezer container, cover and freeze for about 1 hour until firm around the edges.
4. Whisk egg white until stiff. Turn semi-frozen lychee mixture into a bowl and beat to break up the ice crystals. Fold in the egg white, then return to freezer container.
5. Freeze for a further 3–4 hours, until firm. Remove from freezer and place in the refrigerator to soften slightly, about 30 minutes before serving.

Once frozen, use within 2 months.

SPECIAL OCCASION MENUS

VEGETARIAN

Melon With Tomato and Grape Vinaigrette

I frequently get ideas for recipes from meals eaten out, either at friends' houses or restaurants, but this recipe was developed from a starter actually brought to our house for a 'bring-a-course-each' dinner party.

Serves 4
160 Calories a portion

UK	US
2 small Charentais melons	2 small Charentais melons
5cm/2in length of cucumber	2 inch length of cucumber
2 tomatoes	2 tomatoes
100g/4 oz seedless green grapes	4 ounces seedless green grapes

DRESSING:

3 tablespoons olive oil	3 tablespoons olive oil
1 scant tablespoon cider or wine vinegar	1 scant tablespoon cider or wine vinegar
1 teaspoon clear honey	1 teaspoon clear honey
½ teaspoon wholegrain mustard	½ teaspoon wholegrain mustard
small bunch of fresh mint or ¼ teaspoon dried	small bunch of fresh mint or ¼ teaspoon dried
sprigs of fresh mint, or garnish	sprigs of fresh mint, or garnish

1. Halve melons and scoop out seeds. Turn upside down on a plate or cover with film (plastic wrap) to prevent them drying out.
2. Finely dice cucumber and tomatoes and halve grapes. Place in a bowl and cover.
3. Whisk together all the dressing ingredients. Finely chop mint and stir in about 1 tablespoonful. Cover and chill until required.
4. Just before you are ready to serve, whisk the dressing again, pour over the tomato, cucumber and grape mixture and stir lightly together. Spoon into the centre of the melons and serve garnished with sprigs of mint.

Not suitable for freezing.

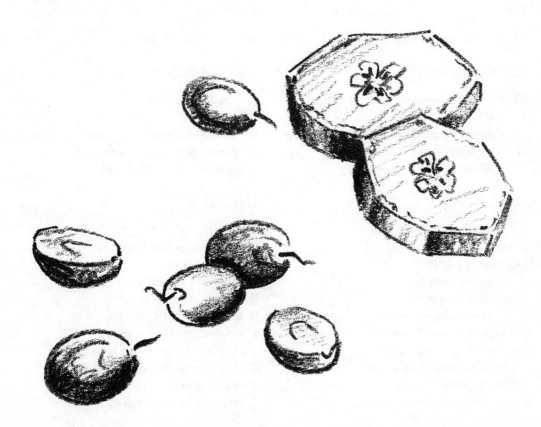

Vegetable Couscous

Couscous is the national dish of Morocco. It is a type of grain (like semolina) steamed above a stew. The complete dish is also called Couscous and it is traditionally cooked in couscoussière. It can be made with chicken, lamb or just vegetables and can be sweet or spicy depending on the flavourings used. Note that the chick-peas require soaking overnight first.

Serves 6
390 Calories a portion

UK

150g/5 oz chick-peas

THE COUSCOUS:

275g/10 oz couscous
450ml/¾ pint water
few drops orange flower water (optional)
¼ teaspoon ground cinnamon
¼ teaspoon ground cloves

THE STEW:

1 large onion
2 tablespoons sunflower oil
1–2 cloves garlic
½ teaspoon paprika
½ teaspoon turmeric
¼ teaspoon chilli powder
1 teaspoon ground cumin
1 teaspoon ground coriander
2 tablespoons tomato purée
4 large carrots
2 parsnips or turnips

US

⅔ cup garbanzo beans

THE COUSCOUS:

1¼ cups couscous
2 cups water
few drops orange flower water (optional)
¼ teaspoon ground cinnamon
¼ teaspoon ground cloves

THE STEW:

1 large onion
2 tablespoons sunflower oil
1–2 cloves garlic
½ teaspoon paprika
½ teaspoon turmeric
¼ teaspoon chilli powder
1 teaspoon ground cumin
1 teaspoon ground coriander
2 tablespoons tomato paste
4 large carrots
2 parsnips or rutabagas

3 large potatoes	3 large potatoes
3 courgettes	3 zucchini
600ml/1 pint vegetable stock	2½ cups vegetable stock
small bunch fresh coriander (optional)	small bunch fresh cilantro (optional)
50g/2 oz sultanas or raisins	⅓ cup raisins
fresh coriander, to garnish	cilantro, to garnish

1. Cover chick-peas (garbanzo beans) with cold water and leave to soak overnight.
2. The following day, drain chick-peas (garbanzo beans) and cover with fresh water in a pan. Bring to the boil, then cook gently for 1 hour.
3. Meanwhile, soak couscous in cold water in a bowl, for about 15 minutes, until the water is absorbed.
4. Slice the onion. Heat the oil in a large saucepan and fry the onion until softened. Crush garlic and add to the onions with all the spices. Cook for 1 minute, then stir in the tomato purée (paste). Take off heat.
5. Peel and cut all the vegetables into large chunks or thick slices. Add all except the courgettes (zucchini) to the pan. Add the drained chick-peas and stock and bring to the boil. Turn down heat.
6. Put the couscous in a steamer and place over the stew. Sprinkle with flower water and spices, then cover tightly and cook gently for 20 minutes.
7. Rougly chop about 2 tablespoons fresh coriander (cilantro).
8. Remove steamer for a moment, add courgettes (zucchini), raisins and coriander to stew. Add a little water if necessary, replace steamer and continue cooking for a further 10 minutes.
9. To serve, tip couscous onto a serving dish and fluff up with a fork. Pile vegetable stew in a mound on top and garnish with sprigs of fresh coriander.

Not suitable for freezing.

SHOPPING NOTE: Couscous is available from large supermarkets and health food shops. If not available, you can substitute long grain rice. Do try and find fresh coriander (cilantro), it has a wonderful flavour, quite different to the dried coriander spice. Try ethnic stores and herb farms as well as large supermarkets.

Baked Stuffed Peaches

An Italian dessert which is especially good made in the summer when fresh peaches are available. At other times of the year, look out for the quality cans of whole peaches, in which the fruit retains a natural almond flavour from the stones left in them. In this recipe, the peaches are stuffed with an almond mixture, then baked in white wine — you can use unsweetened orange juice if preferred. Serve warm with Greek strained yogurt or low-fat fromage frais.

Serves 6
175 Calories a portion (without yogurt)

UK

6 whole ripe peaches
75g/3 oz ground almonds
40g/1½ oz fresh wholewheat
  breadcrumbs
40g/1½ oz caster sugar
1 orange
125ml/4 fl oz dry white wine

US

6 whole ripe peaches
¾ cup ground almonds
¾ cup fresh wholewheat breadcrumbs
3 tablespoons superfine sugar
1 orange
½ cup dry white wine

1. Halve peaches and remove stones. Scoop out a little of the flesh to make the hollows slightly larger, reserving the flesh.
2. Mix together the almonds, breadcrumbs, sugar and peach flesh.
3. Grate rind from orange and squeeze juice and add both to almond mixture. Mix in 1 tablespoon of the wine.
4. Place peaches in a shallow ovenproof dish and spoon the almond mixture into the peach centres. Pour remaining wine around the peaches.
5. Bake at 180°C/350°F/Gas Mark 4 for about 25 minutes, until the peaches are tender. Allow less time if using canned fruit. Serve hot.

Not suitable for freezing.

INDIAN

Tomatoes Stuffed with Spinach

A lovely colourful starter. Do buy good-sized Continental or beefsteak tomatoes so there's plenty of room inside for the spicy spinach mixture.

Serves 6
90 Calories a portion

UK	US
6 large tomatoes	6 large tomatoes
1 onion	1 onion
2 cloves garlic	2 cloves garlic
575g/1¼ lb fresh spinach	1¼ pound fresh spinach
1 chilli pepper	1 green chilli pepper
small piece fresh root ginger	small piece fresh root ginger
2 tablespoons sunflower oil	2 tablespoons sunflower oil
2 teaspoons garam masala	2 teaspoons garam masala

1. Cut the tops off the tomatoes, scoop out the seeds and pulp, chop and reserve.
2. Finely chop onion and crush garlic. Trim and finely shred spinach. Finely chop chilli pepper, discarding the seeds and peel and finely chop ginger.
3. Heat the oil in a pan, add the onion and garlic and cook until softened. Stir in the chilli and ginger, then the spinach. Let it cook down for a minute, then add the reserved chopped tomato pulp and garam masala. Cover and cook gently for 5 minutes.
4. Spoon the spinach mixture into the tomatoes and place in an ovenproof dish. Bake for 15–20 minutes at 180°C/350°F/Gas Mark 4, until the tomatoes have softened but still retain their shape.

Not suitable for freezing.

Lamb Biryani

A wonderfully spicy Indian dish of partly cooked rice and curry layered and baked together. It is a meal in itself but should be served with a yogurt raita (see recipes on page 44 and page 101) and a diced cucumber and tomato side salad. Authentically basmati rice should be used, but brown rice works well and provides higher fibre value.

Serves 6
495 Calories a portion

UK

1 large onion
2 cloves garlic
small piece fresh root ginger
675g/1½ lb lean lamb
2 tablespoons sunflower oil
6 cardamom pods
2 teaspoons ground cumin
2 teaspoons ground coriander
½ teaspoon chilli powder
6 cloves
1 cinnamon stick
2 bay leaves
½ teaspoon whole black peppercorns
1 lemon
3 tomatoes
150ml/¼ pint water

RICE:

pinch of saffron strands
2 tablespoons warm milk
275g/10 oz brown rice
1 small onion
1 tablespoon sunflower oil

US

1 large onion
2 cloves garlic
small pieces fresh root ginger
1½ pound lean lamb
2 tablespoons sunflower oil
6 cardamom pods
2 teaspoons ground cumin
2 teaspoons ground coriander
½ teaspoon chilli powder
6 cloves
1 cinnamon stick
2 bay leaves
½ teaspoon whole black peppercorns
1 lemon
3 tomatoes
⅔ cup water

RICE:

pinch of saffron strands
2 tablespoons warm milk
1¼ cups brown rice
1 small onion
1 tablespoon sunflower oil

750ml/1¼ pints water
few drops rose water (optional)

3 cups water
few drops rose water (optional)

GARNISH:

GARNISH:

shelled pistachio nuts (unsalted)
sultanas
fresh coriander

shelled pistachio nuts (unsalted)
golden seedless raisins
cilantro

1. Chop the onion. Crush the garlic. Peel and finely mince the ginger. Cut lamb into bite-sized cubes, trimming away any visible fat.
2. Heat the oil in a large saucepan and cook the onion until softened. Stir in the garlic and ginger and cook for a further minute. Add lamb and fry until browned all over.
3. Crush cardamoms and discard pods. Add seeds to the pan with all the other spices and stir around.
4. Squeeze juice from lemon. Chop tomatoes. Add to pan together with water. Cover and cook gently for 1 hour.
5. Meanwhile add the saffron to the milk and leave to stand. Rince rice in a sieve (wire mesh colander) under cold running water.
6. Slice onion, then fry in the oil until softened. Stir in the rice, then pour in water and saffron liquid. Bring to the boil and cook for 30 minutes, by which time all the liquid should be absorbed.
7. Layer the rice and lamb in an ovenproof dish, then cover and cook at 170°C/325°F/Gas Mark 3 for 30 minutes, by which time the lamb should be tender and the whole dish beautifully succulent.
8. Sprinkle a few drops of rose water over the top, then scatter over some pistachio nuts and sultanas (raisins). Garnish further with some coriander leaves (cilantro).

May be frozen. Use within 2 months.
Thaw overnight in the refrigerator, then reheat gently in a covered dish in a moderate oven. Garnish as above.

Mango and Passion Fruit Fool_____

Both mangoes and passion fruit are intensely fragrant, the mangoes also having a slightly spicy quality. Together they produce a wonderful flavour, and make a divine fool. The fruits are simply puréed, then blended with custard and yogurt. This fruit fool looks spectacular decorated with some exotic flower blooms.

Serves 6
165 Calories a portion

UK

300ml/½ pint semi-skimmed milk
2 egg yolks
2 tablespoons cornflour
40g/1½ oz caster sugar
2 ripe mangoes
4 passion fruit
175ml/6 fl oz Greek strained yogurt

US

1¼ cups low-fat milk
2 egg yolks
2 tablespoons cornstarch
3 tablespoons superfine sugar
2 ripe mangoes
4 passion fruit
¾ cup Greek strained yogurt

1. First make the custard. Blend together 1 tablespoon of the milk with the egg yolks and cornflour (cornstarch). Heat the rest of the milk until just boiling. Stir hot milk into the egg yolk mixture, then return to pan and continue to heat, stirring all the time, until thickened. (It will be quite thick.) Remove from heat, stir in sugar, then leave to cool.
2. Peel and stone the mangoes and place flesh in a food processor or blender. Halve passion fruit, scoop out flesh into the mangoes. Process or blend until smooth. If not completely smooth, push through a sieve (wire mesh colander).
3. Blend together fruit purée and custard and about two-thirds of the yogurt.

4. Divide mixture between 6 individual sundae dishes, then swirl a little of the remaining yogurt into each.

Not suitable for freezing.

BRITISH CONTEMPORARY

Sophie's Salad

I named this salad after my little daughter because it's made of four of her favourite foods: avocado, kiwi fruit, pears and cucumber. Being different shades of green, they look very pretty, sliced and artistically arranged on individual serving plates with a light herb yogurt dressing drizzled over. The dressing can be made in advance, but the salads should be prepared shortly before serving to be really fresh.

Serves 6
185 Calories a portion

UK

300ml/½ pint natural low-fat yogurt
1 tablespoon wine vinegar
2 teaspoons dill sauce (or 2 teaspoons
   wholegrain mustard and some dill
   weed)
small bunch fresh parsley and tarragon
freshly ground black pepper
2 large avocados
2 ripe pears
1 lemon
2–3 kiwi fruit
½ cucumber
head of curly endive
bunch of watercress

US

1¼ cups plain low-fat yogurt
1 tablespoon wine vinegar
2 teaspoons dill sauce (or 2 teaspoons
   wholegrain mustard and some dill
   weed)
small bunch fresh parsley and tarragon
freshly ground black pepper
2 large avocados
2 ripe pears
1 lemon
2–3 kiwi fruit
½ cucumber
head of chicory
bunch of watercress

1. First make up the dressing. Stir the vinegar and dill sauce (or mustard) into the yogurt. Chop parsley, tarragon and dill if using, and stir about 1 tablespoon of each into the yogurt. Season with pepper.
2. Peel and stone the avocados, then slice neatly. Peel, core and slice the pears. Squeeze lemon juice over both.

3. Peel and slice kiwi fruit into rounds. Using a cannula knife or vegetable peeler, remove thin strips of peel lengthways from the cucumber to produce a striped effect, then slice cucumber into rounds. Cut into the centre of each cucumber and kiwi slice, so you can turn them into twists.
4. Make a bed of curly endive (chicory) on each serving plate, then arrange avocados, pears, kiwi and cucumber slices on top. Drizzle over dressing and garnish with sprigs of watercress. Serve immediately.

Not suitable for freezing.

Monkfish Provençale

Monkfish, although quite expensive, is a particularly good choice of fish if you're normally put off by bones, as it contains one central bone which can be easily removed. It is also firm textured and doesn't break up when it is cooked. Ask your fishmonger (dealer) to skin and bone it for you. Serve with brown rice and a lightly-cooked green vegetable.

Serves 6
225 Calories a portion

UK	US
1 large onion	1 large onion
2 cloves garlic	2 cloves garlic
675g/1½ lb tomatoes	1½ pounds tomatoes
1kg/2¼ lb monkfish tail	2¼ pounds monkfish tail
3 tablespoons olive oil	3 tablespoons olive oil
3 tablespoons tomato purée	3 tablespoons tomato paste
175ml/6 fl oz dry white wine	¾ cup dry white wine
freshly ground black pepper	freshly ground black pepper
pinch of sugar	pinch of sugar
parsley	parsley

1. Chop the onion and crush the garlic. Skin and chop the tomatoes. Skin and bone fish (unless already prepared for you) then cut up into large cubes.
2. Heat the oil in a pan and gently cook the onion until softened. Stir in the garlic and tomatoes and cook gently for about 5 minutes more, until the tomatoes have softened down.
3. Add the purée (paste), wine and seasoning, bring to the boil, then turn down heat. Add fish, cover and simmer gently for about 10 minutes, or until the fish is tender.
4. Chop 2–3 tablespoons of parsley and stir in to fish. Serve immediately.

Not suitable for freezing.

Raspberry Cranachan

A Scottish dessert for a special occasion, made with toasted oatmeal, 'cream' (low-fat type), whisky (or rum) and raspberries. Raspberry growing is a big industry in Scotland and the fruit has a particularly exquisite flavour. Blackberries or a mixture of the two berries could be substituted.

Serves 6
205 Calories a portion

UK

50g/2 oz porridge oats
285ml/½ pint low-fat Double 'cream'
150ml/¼ pint natural low-fat yogurt
2 teaspoons whisky or dark rum
   (optional)
few drops vanilla essence
1 tablespoon caster sugar
350g/12 oz fresh raspberries

US

½ cup rolled oats
1¼ cups low-fat Double 'cream'
⅔ cup plain low-fat yogurt
2 teaspoons whisky or dark rum
   (optional)
few drops vanilla essence
1 tablespoon superfine sugar
12 ounces fresh raspberries

1. Spread oats on a baking sheet and brown under the grill. Allow to cool.
2. Whip 'cream' until just thickened then fold in yogurt. Lightly stir in whisky (or rum), vanilla essence (extract) and sugar to taste, then most of the toasted oats, reserving a couple of tablespoonfuls.
3. Divide raspberries between 6 individual glass dishes, reserving 18 nice berries for decoration. Pile 'cream' mixture on top then sprinkle with reserved oats. Place 3 raspberries on each. Serve chilled.

Not suitable for freezing.

CHINESE

Oriental Fish Parcels

Steaming food in little parcels not only seals in the flavour and goodness of the ingredients but provides an attractive and unusual way of serving a starter. The parcels contain a mixture of white fish and prawns with sliced baby corn, mangetout (snow peas) and bitter-sweet, tangy kumquats for colour and appeal. The parcels can be made of greaseproof paper (baking parchment) or aluminium foil, although personally I think paper parcels look prettier.

Serves 6
125 Calories a portion

UK	US
6 kumquats	6 kumquats
6 baby corn	6 baby corn
50g/2 oz mangetout	1 cup snow peas
3 spring onions	3 scallions (green onions)
225g/8 oz white fish fillet	8 ounces white fish fillet
small piece of fresh root ginger	small piece of fresh root ginger
225g/8 oz shelled prawns	8 ounces shelled prawns
1 tablespoon sesame oil	1 tablespoon sesame oil
1 tablespoon dry sherry	1 tablespoon dry sherry
freshly ground black pepper	freshly ground black pepper
lime wedges and spring onion brushes to garnish (see note)	lime wedges and spring onion brushes to garnish

1. First cut out 6 × 25cm/10 in squares of double–thickness greaseproof paper (baking parchment) or foil.
2. Thinly slice the kumquats, baby corn, mangetout and spring onions. Slice the white fish into thin strips, removing any skin and bone. Peel and finely chop ginger.
3. Divide the fish, prawns, fruit and vegetables between the squares of paper.

148

4. Blend together oil, sherry and ginger, and season with pepper. Sprinkle a little over the contents of each parcel. Fold parcels into envelopes, tucking in the flaps to secure.

5. Arrange parcels in a steamer and cook for 5–10 minutes, just before serving. Serve the wrapped parcels on plates garnished with lime wedges and spring onions brushes. (See below).

Not suitable for freezing.

COOK'S NOTE: To make spring onion brushes, trim green tops and roots, so onions are only about 10cm/4 in long. Carefully shred the top, leaving the base intact. Place in a bowl of iced water for at least 30 minutes, until the green ends curl.

Lemon Chicken With Cashew Nuts_____

I have frequently prepared this dish for dinner parties and it's always popular. It's a favourite of mine, too, because I can prepare the ingredients in advance, and cook it quickly at the last minute. I like to serve it with brown rice and lightly steamed vegetables.

Serves 6
295 Calories a portion

UK

4 large, boned chicken breasts
small piece fresh root ginger
1 fat clove garlic
2 egg whites
2 teaspoons cornflour

SAUCE:

2 lemons
2 teaspoons cornflower
2 teaspoons sugar
1 tablespoon light soy sauce
1 tablespoon dry sherry
150ml/¼ pint chicken stock
2 tablespoons sunflower oil
1 tablespoon sesame oil
50g/2 oz cashew nuts

GARNISH:

lemon slices
fresh coriander

US

4 large, boned chicken breasts (raw)
small piece fresh root ginger
1 fat clove garlic
2 egg whites
2 teaspoons cornstarch

SAUCE:

2 lemons
2 teaspoons cornstarch
2 teaspoons sugar
1 tablespoon light soy sauce
1 tablespoon dry sherry
⅔ cup chicken stock
2 tablespoons sunflower oil
1 tablespoon sesame oil
½ cup cashew nuts

GARNISH:

lemon slices
cilantro

1. Slice the chicken, across the grain, into thin strips.
2. Peel and finely chop the ginger. Crush the garlic. Lightly beat the egg whites, just to break them up, then mix in the ginger, garlic and cornflour (cornstarch). Stir the

chicken into this mixture, then cover and place in the refrigerator.

3. For the sauce, squeeze the juice from the lemons into a jug. Blend in the cornflour (cornstarch), sugar, soy sauce, sherry and stock.

4. .Just before you're ready to serve, arrange the slices of lemon around the outside of the serving dish. Heat both the oils in a wok or large frying pan (skillet). Add the chicken in the egg white mixture and stir fr⋅ ⋅ a high heat for about 5 minutes, until the chicken is cooked. Remove chickeı. ⋅ plate covered with kitchen towel (paper) to drain.

5. Add the cashew nuts to the pan and toss quickly until golden, then remove.

6. Wipe out the pan with a piece of kitchen paper. Stir the sauce in the jug, then pour into the pan and heat, stirring continuously until thickened.

7. Return chicken to the pan and heat through in the sauce. Lastly stir in nuts, then serve on your prepared dish garnished with coriander (cilantro).

Not suitable for freezing.

Almond Jelly With Exotic Fruits

Almond jelly is a classic Chinese dessert and looks very appealing served with a refreshing selection of slightly more unusual fruits. The pink jewel-like seeds of the pomegranate look exceedingly pretty.

Serves 6
125 Calories a portion

UK

JELLY

600ml/1 pint semi-skimmed milk
2 tablespoons powdered gelatine
2 tablespoons caster sugar
1 teaspoon almond essence

FRUIT SALAD:

6 lychees
3 kiwi fruit
3 clementines or oranges
1 star fruit
1 pomegranate
90ml/3 fl oz unsweetened fruit juice

US

JELLY

2½ cups low-fat milk
2 tablespoons powdered gelatine
2 tablespoons sugar
1 teaspoon almond extract

FRUIT SALAD:

6 lychees
3 kiwi fruit
3 clementines or oranges
1 star fruit
1 pomegranate
⅓ cup unsweetened fruit juice

1. Warm a quarter of the milk, then take off the heat and stir in the gelatine. If it doesn't quite dissolve, return to heat and warm gently until it does, stirring until the time. Be careful not to over-heat.
2. Heat the rest of the milk with the sugar until the sugar dissolves. Take off heat and stir in almond essence (extract). Stir this milk into the dissolved gelatine mixture.
3. Pour into a wetted, decorative 600ml/1 pint (2½ cup) mould and leave to set in the refrigerator for abour 2 hours.
4. Peel and cut up all the fruit. Cut open pomegranate and remove seeds. Put the fruit into the fruit juice to keep it moist.

5. Turn out jelly on to a large flat platter and surround with the fruit, scattering some of the pomegranate seeds over the jelly.

Not suitable for freezing.

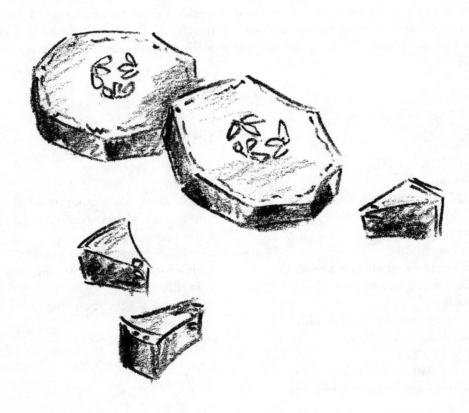

FRENCH

Mixed Hors D'Oeuvres

I always think there is nothing to beat this as a starter, and it is my favourite choice when I am in France. It is traditionally an array of various salads, cold meats, marinated fish, from which you can make your own selection. In this recipe, and to keep the salt level down, I have chosen only vegetable ingredients. It makes a colourful and tempting first course which can be prepared ahead and assembled at the last minute. I like to use the Italian balsamic vinegar for this; although expensive its flavour is so good that you only need to use a little of it. Balsamic vinegar is made from concentrated, fermented grape juice.

Serves 6
145 Calories a portion

UK	**US**
350g/12 oz celeriac	12 ounces celeriac
1 lemon	1 lemon
1 tablespoon wholegrain mustard	1 tablespoon wholegrain mustard
175ml/6 fl oz natural Greek strained yogurt	⅔ cup plain Greek strained yogurt
1 dill cucumber	1 dill cucumber
2–3 ready-to-eat cooked beetroot	2–3 ready-to-eat cooked beets
1 tablespoon balsamic or wine vinegar (optional)	1 tablespoon balsamic or wine vinegar (optional)
2–3 spring onions or a few chives	2–3 scallions (green onions) or a few chives
small bunch of parsley	small bunch of parsley

Carrot Salad with Mint and Cumin (see page 105)
some nice mixed leaves, to garnish

1. Peel and finely grate the celeriac, then squeeze over lemon juice, toss and leave to soften. (The lemon juice also prevents the celeriac from discolouring). Stir the mustard into the yogurt. Finely chop cucumber and stir into the yogurt. Stir celeriac into yogurt mixture, cover and refrigerate.
2. Cut beetroot (beets) into small dice. (If not using the ready-to-eat type, peel and trim first, then dice.) Moisten with vinegar. Finely slice spring onions (scallions) or chives and chop a couple of tablespoons of parsley. Toss both into beetroot, cover and chill.
3. Make up the Carrot Salad following the recipe on page 105.
4. Just before you're ready to serve, arrange the three salads in contrasting rows on serving plates. Garnish with salad leaves. Serve with warm, crusty wholemeal bread (look out for wholewheat French baguettes.)

Not suitable for freezing.

Pork With Prunes

This is a classic French recipe which I've frequently served at dinner parties because it's always well received yet so simple to prepare. Traditionally the recipe uses cream but natural yogurt works very well as a low fat and lower calorie substitute.

Serves 6   430 Calories a portion

UK

350g/12 oz no-need-to-soak dried prunes
450ml/¾ pint dry white wine
6 lean pork steaks
1 tablespoon sunflower oil
25g/1 oz polyunsaturated margarine
1 tablespoon redcurrant jelly
freshly ground black pepper
1 tablespoon cornflour
200ml/7 fl oz natural low-fat yogurt
fresh parsley, to garnish

US

2½ cups no-need-to-soak dried prunes
2 cups dry white wine
6 lean pork steaks
1 tablespoon sunflower oil
2½ tablespoons polyunsaturated
  margarine
1 tablespoon redcurrant jelly
freshly ground black pepper
1 tablespoon cornstarch
¾ cup plain low-fat yogurt
fresh parsley, to garnish

1. Place prunes in a jug or bowl and pour over wine.
2. Trim any fat from pork. Heat oil and margarine in a large pan (skillet), add the pork and fry until browned on both sides. Drain off any excess fat.
3. Pour in wine and prunes, add jelly and season with pepper. Bring to the boil, then turn down heat, cover and cook gently for about 20 minutes.
4. Blend cornflour (cornstarch) with the yogurt. Chop some parsley.
5. Lift out pork and prunes onto a warmed serving dish and cover to keep warm. Gradually stir the yogurt into the liquid in the pan, stirring continuously over the heat until thoroughly blended and heated through. Pour over pork and prunes and serve sprinkled with parsley.

Not suitable for freezing.

Iles Flottantes

This recipe has always been a favourite. Its English name is Floating Islands and is simply poached meringues on a real vanilla custard sauce. Serve it with fresh strawberries.

Serves 6   175 Calories a portion (without strawberries)

UK

3 fresh eggs
75g/3 oz caster sugar
1 tablespoon cornflour
½ teaspoon pure vanilla essence
600ml/1 pint semi-skimmed milk
25g/1 oz flaked almonds
fresh strawberries, to serve

US

3 fresh eggs
½ cup sugar
1 tablespoon cornstarch
½ teaspoon pure vanilla extract
2½ cups low-fat milk
¼ cup slivered almonds
fresh strawberries, to serve

1. Separate the eggs and blend the yolks with a third of the sugar, the cornflour (cornstarch) and vanilla.
2. Heat the milk to boiling point, then stir it into the egg yolk mixture. Return to the pan and heat very gently, stirring all the time, until thickened.
3. Pour custard into shallow serving dish/six individual dishes and leave to cool.
4. Now make the meringues. Whisk the egg whites until stiff, then gradually whisk in the remaining sugar.
5. Fill about two thirds of a frying pan (skillet) with boiling water. Turn down heat so that it is just simmering, then gently lower in tablespoonfuls of meringue. Try to achieve neat egg shapes. Put in just a few at a time so they don't knock together. Poach gently for 5 minutes, carefully turning them half-way through the cooking time. Lift out, using a draining spoon, on to kitchen paper. Continue until all the meringue has been cooked.
6. Toast almonds on a baking sheet under the grill and hull strawberries.
7. Place meringues on the custard and chill. Just before serving, scatter over the almonds. Decorate with a few strawberries and serve the rest in a separate bowl.

Not suitable for freezing.

Body Mass Index Chart

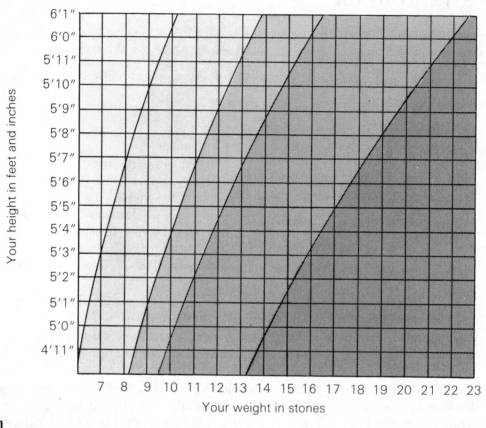

Underweight. Are you eating enough?

OK. This is the desirable weight range for health.

Overweight. Not likely to have much effect on your health but don't get any fatter!

Fat. Your health could suffer if you don't lose weight.

Very fat. This is severe and treatment is urgently required.

From GARROW J.S. (1981) *Treat Obesity Seriously*. Edinburgh: Churchill Livingstone.

INDEX

159

160